BRUCE HELMER'S

SUCCESSFUL FINANCIAL PLANNING:

DISPELLING MYTHS, FALLACIES, AND OUTRIGHT DECEPTIONS ABOUT YOUR FINANCIAL FUTURE

BRUCE HELMER, RFC

specialtypress
PUBLISHERS AND WHOLESALERS

Bruce Helmer's Successful Financial Planning: Dispelling Myths, Fallacies, and Outright Deceptions About Your Financial Future

by Bruce W. Helmer

ISBN: 1-58007-043-4

Copyright © 2000, Bruce W. Helmer

For additional copies of this work, contact:
Specialty Press, 11605 Kost Dam Rd.
North Branch, MN 55056, 651-583-3239
800-895-4585

Library of Congress Cataloging-in-Publication Data

Helmer, Bruce W. , 1959-
    Bruce Helmer's successful financial planning : dispelling myths, fallacies,
    and outright deceptions about your financial future / by Bruce W. Helmer.
        p. cm.
    ISBN 1-58007-043-4 (softcover)
    1. Finance, Personal—United States. 2. Investments—United States.

HG179.H3876 2000
332.024—dc21   00–046346

WEALTH
ENHANCEMENT
GROUP

Securities and investment advice offered through FSC SECURITIES CORPORATION, a Registered Broker/Dealer (Member NASD & SIPC) and a Registered Investment Advisor.

DEDICATION

I wish to dedicate this book to my family. My wife Laura should probably be listed as co-author. At the very least she should receive credit for word processing, proofreading, and editing. Without her love, patience, wisdom, understanding, and most of all, *help*, I would have been unable to do this project.

Also, I want to say to my kids, if the writing of this book was ever the cause of any lack of attention on my part or has any other detrimental impact, I am truly sorry. Nothing is more important to me than my family. I know you are too young to understand this, but it is my hope that when you're older you will appreciate what I have done and be half as proud of me as I am of you.

ACKNOWLEDGMENT

I would like to thank my partners Jerry Bernard, Madeleine Bernard, David Hess, Mark Beethe, John Castino, and Morgan Schleif, and the entire staff at Wealth Enhancement Group. These people have helped my professional growth tremendously and I am convinced there isn't a better group of people working together anywhere. Also, thanks to Dave Smith for his help and guidance. Special thanks to my assistant, Ann Wold, and my wife Laura[1] for trying to keep me organized.

---

[1] I know I thanked her already, but she's worth thanking twice.

BRUCE W. HELMER is a Registered Financial Consultant and President of Wealth Enhancement Group. Dedicated financial professionals, the Wealth Enhancement Group manages more than $450 million in client assets and provides comprehensive wealth management services with an emphasis on tax efficiency.

Before joining the Wealth Enhancement Group, Bruce was President and Senior Asset Coordinator for a local financial consulting firm. Prior to that position, he spent six years in the banking industry.

Bruce is a 1981 graduate of the University of Minnesota, Morris with a Bachelor of Arts degree in Social Science. His post-graduate financial education includes pursuits in Certified Financial Planning, Chartered Financial Consulting, Wealth Strategies, and the Economics of Wealth.

A frequent lecturer on personal financial issues, Bruce has also developed and taught numerous courses for other financial professionals as well as the public. Bruce can be heard discussing personal finance issues and answering call-in questions on his weekly radio show on WCCO 830AM in the Minneapolis area.

Bruce and his team can be reached at:

Wealth Enhancement Group
125 West Lake Street, Suite 200
Wayzata, MN 55391
(800) 492-1222
fax (952) 449-4886
www.wealthenhancement.com

TABLE OF CONTENTS

INTRODUCTION

So much financial and investment advice on TV and radio, in magazines and books, and overheard around the Starbucks counter is wrong for you. We hear some of it so often, aided by the marketing dollars of financial and investment institutions with very deep pockets, that it becomes conventional wisdom. And nothing could be more detrimental, even dangerous, to your financial future than conventional wisdom, because much of it is based in myth and some of it is simply deceptive.

I urge you to set your goals higher than you could achieve if you accepted conventional wisdom—or took as gospel the marketing messages that many financial and investment institutions impart relentlessly. The fact that you are reading a book on financial planning tells me that you are not the typical American who has saved too little and given too little thought to his or her financial future. You want better than the Average Joe or Jolene—and you can get it.

But you can't do better than average if you think of yourself and your financial future as average. You can't follow conventional wisdom. You can't take the advice that's often intended for people who have never given a serious thought to how they can make their lives better by carefully planning to meet their financial goals. When it comes to saving and investing, averages rarely apply to individuals.

It doesn't matter if you have $500 in savings or $5 million, you can optimize your resources to help you get what you want out of life—you can be wealthy. But that will never happen if you fall victim to the myths, fallacies, and outright lies that are often dispensed as wisdom or truth.

■ WHO WANTS TO BE WEALTHY?

Since the beginning of time, different cultures have established different methods of measuring or identifying wealth. Typically, however, wealth has to do with possessions and in most cultures being wealthy has been preferred to not being wealthy.

But when I talk about wealth, I'm not necessarily talking about the accumulation of money. Being wealthy doesn't mean that you amass huge sums of money that you squeeze tightly until you die. I'm talking instead about living a rich life—rich in the things you value and enjoy. That may mean you want money to support your lifestyle. That may mean you want money to make a better life for your children and grandchildren. That may mean you want to use your money to combat society's problems. That may mean you want to be able to pursue your passions, to do those things you've always wanted to do. That may mean you simply want the security of having money in reserve to cover unexpected costs—a freedom from worry. And living a rich life may mean that you want to have the resources to propagate your beliefs—religious, social, cultural, or political.

In nearly twenty years of advising people how to enhance their wealth, I have seen every one of those motivations. People desire wealth for a multitude of reasons—and I respect each individual's right to choose what to do with his or her life and wealth. Our motivations are very complicated and I do not judge the reasons any person tries to enhance wealth.

But that is always where I start as I get to know prospective clients: I ask them about their dreams, what they would most like to do with their lives. Without exception, the pursuit of a life imagined, the pursuit of lifelong goals is aided by intelligent efforts to optimize resources, to enhance wealth. To me enhancing wealth means enriching life in whatever way you choose—without regard to the size of your bank account or investment portfolio.

■ WHAT DO YOU NEED TO KNOW?

Reading this book will give you an opportunity—the opportunity to reclaim power over your finances from large financial institutions and exercise it yourself. I want your money to work as hard for you as you work for your money!

A famous educator once said, "Much of knowledge is indeed merely memory and this is why so many misconceptions persist for such a long time. For example, science is rife with error. Because so many people are so thoroughly schooled in the common misconceptions, however, only the most brilliantly skeptical of them ever discover a mistake. And even then, it will likely be denied for generations to come." Until Columbus made his famous journey, for how long did people think the world was flat?

Knowledge for most people is memorizing what someone has taught them. They have not been schooled in how to think or use common sense. True knowledge is a function of the ability to reason and solve problems without bias or preconceived ideas. Don't neglect the exercise of your brain in order to follow the masses—especially when it comes to your dreams and your money.

A perfect example is the prevailing attitudes toward personal finance. Most people make their financial decisions based on the rationale, "That's what everyone else is doing." When it comes to financial matters, most people behave like lemmings following one another over the cliff to their doom. This book could help you take a different path—and save you from going over the cliff.

My purpose is to challenge prevailing attitudes about personal finance and encourage you to think—really think—about what you want from your life and how personal financial planning can help you get what you want.

Wealth doesn't come easy. Nearly everyone wants it; most people just don't know how to get it. And there's competition. Money is always in short supply. In healthy economies, with governments that don't print it like tissue paper, there's never enough money to satisfy everyone's dreams. If enhancing wealth were easy, it wouldn't be valued. Whether in art, sports, entertainment, or nature, we value most that which is rare—talent, beauty, and, yes, money.

Some of that competition for money even comes directly from those who are trying to advise you what to do with your money or how to get more, such as financial institutions and investment firms. But what works best for them, what makes them money, may not be what works for you. So you have to be very cautious from whom you take advice. The same goes for financial service professionals like me. Yes, I want to be wealthy. But I think I can achieve my personal goals precisely by advising people to be skeptical about traditional thinking in financial matters. I think I can achieve my goals by helping you achieve yours.

■ WHY ME?

Why should you believe me? Good question! If you're asking yourself that, you're already on the right track—challenge everything.

I've been in the financial services industry for 18 years. I began by dispensing much of the same advice that I advise against in this book. Over the years, however, I began to see that much of the standard advice wasn't very good. It either wasn't successful or didn't apply to the situations of clients I was seeing every day.

The more clients I met who were in vastly different financial situations, but embraced the same concepts, the more I realized how deeply some conventional wisdom was ingrained in our collective psyche. So I began to be skeptical of that wisdom and looked more closely at where it came from, who promoted it, who stood to gain from it. My skepticism nearly turned to cynicism as I saw over time how badly conventional wisdom served so many people—but how well it served the established institutions of finance and investing.

I also had to overcome my natural conservatism on financial matters. Growing up in rural Minnesota, in an agricultural economy, I learned the value of staying with the tried and true. Farmers can't try every newfangled notion that comes along, because they get only one chance each year, in most cases, to plant and harvest a crop. What they do better work, because they won't have a chance to correct a mistake until next year. Change occurs gradually and collective wisdom has great validity.

That said, I know many farmers and rural businessmen who are very progressive in their thinking on financial and agricultural matters. There are several important similarities in the two disciplines, most noticeably the concept of allocation of assets, which I will talk about at length in Chapter 2 and throughout the book. Investors allocate assets to different types of investments, farmers allocate acreage to different crops, both with the goal of increasing returns. You may be wondering why I didn't use a farm colloquialism and write, "They don't put all their eggs in one basket." I didn't because the goal of asset allocation goes well beyond reducing risk. Much, much more on that in a moment.

My exposure to the questions and comments of thousands of radio listeners—my show has become the top-rated program in its time period—has reinforced for me that many people are not doing as well as they could financially because they accept as truth several key financial principles that in fact are not true or at least do not apply to everyone. The important myths, fallacies, and lies that were preventing people from enhancing their wealth became more glaring and infuriating than ever.

I would also be remiss if I didn't mention the significant role my partners at Wealth Enhancement Group have played in refining my thinking on finance and investing. They are very smart people who enjoy unconventional analysis. Their constant questions and challenges have reinforced my own—to the gain of our clients.

Instead of letting cynicism take hold—I don't think anyone who knows me would call me cynical—and letting the wisdom of the past dominate my thinking, I opted to take advantage of the opportunity presented by the failing conventional wisdom all around

me and recommend different courses. Both for my clients and for anyone else who was truly concerned about their financial future and who would listen or read.

I decided to do what I could to shoot down those myths in this book. This book is organized around several widely held myths that could be harmful to you if you accept them. Many people, including many powerful people in respected financial institutions, will tell you some of my ideas are crazy. I urge you to listen to their criticisms carefully and determine for yourself whose arguments make sense—and whose are based on ulterior motives or hidden agendas. Whenever you hear an argument over how to save or make money, always consider who stands to gain if you follow one course of action or another.

Not everyone who disagrees with me is being dishonest. In any field, honorable people can disagree. And some of the myths I attack may make sense for some people. The question is "Do they make sense for you?"

Are my clients all wealthy now thanks to my change of mind and advice? Certainly not, but I think that I can safely say that most of my clients are satisfied with the advice I've provided. Of the thousands of clients I have advised, many have only implemented our strategies in recent years, so they are not all wealthy—yet.

■ MYTHS, FALLACIES, AND LIES

Some of the more popular—and more harmful—traditional financial myths, fallacies, and lies that I intend to shoot down include:

- Create a financial plan to meet your projected *needs*. False! Embraced by too many people, it actually limits your potential.

- The key to achieving your goals is picking the right stock. False! Overemphasis on investment *products* is dangerous. Investment *strategies* are far more important.

- Fixed-interest investments are stable and safe. Dangerously false. They can actually be as volatile as the stock market.

- Compounding interest in taxable instruments is a good deal. Very wrong! Nearly everyone does it, but it is absolutely inefficient.

- Pay off debt as fast as you can. Not all debt! Some debt can be very positive.

- Buy stocks more cheaply by dollar-cost averaging. False. It's vastly overrated as an investment strategy.

- Invest as much as you can in pretax retirement plans. No! While pretax plans are good for some, for others they are a very bad use of money.

- You need some life insurance, but it's a bad investment. Totally wrong. No one needs it—but many want it for good reason: it can be a very smart investment.

- It's a waste of money to hire professionals to help you create an efficient plan for your money. Very shortsighted. The complexities of investing, especially tax implications, make the creation and implementation of an efficient financial plan too difficult or too time-consuming for most people.

- The result of making charitable contributions is that you do good or feel good. True! But the impact of charitable gifts can have significant economic benefits for the giver, too.

■ IF YOU DON'T WANT TO READ ANY FURTHER

If you've read this far in a super bookstore while sitting in a comfy chair and have no intention of actually buying this book, let me give you some quick tips before you move on to the New Fiction shelf or go see if your kids' story time is over.

If you do nothing else, take to heart and put to work these 10 keys to personal finance. There's a lot more to learn in the pages that follow, but these are the bare bones. Do these things and you'll probably accumulate more wealth than you ever thought you would.

On the other hand, if you do read the whole book, keep these 10 keys in mind as you consider everything else I've written, all the sacred cows I dispatch, and all the blasphemy I dispense—or so my critics will say.

10 KEYS TO SUCCESS IN PERSONAL FINANCE

1. **Take action.** Most people wait too long to start. Time is your biggest ally.

2. **Set goals.** Target saving 10% of your adjusted gross income. Try to visualize your life when you retire.

3. **Use credit wisely.** Credit cards are a convenience, not an efficient way to borrow money. Pay cash or pay with credit cards only when you have the cash available to pay off your balance each month. Shop for credit: interest rate, deductibility, and duration. Use home equity credit if you can.

4. **Invest in yourself and your family.** Education, self-improvement, your business. These are all investments that will pay a greater return, financially and in terms of your happiness, than most savings plans. I include protection products in this category: disability, liability, and life insurance; wills; and proper legal work.

5. **Own your own home.** A home is one of the best investments you can make for your financial and emotional well-being.

6. **Invest the majority of your money in vehicles with long-term appreciation potential**— stocks, real estate, your own business—rather than putting your money in fixed-interest investments.

7. **Avoid emotional investment decisions.** Create a strategy and stick to it. Revise it as necessary, but stick to it. Don't get caught up in the emotional frenzy of chasing greater and greater returns. What's hot in investing now can go cold in a hurry.

8. **Work with your spouse.** About 50% of marriages end in divorce. Disagreements over money are often cited as a primary cause.

9. **Be patient.** Get-rich-quick schemes rarely succeed. Perseverance and consistency pay off.

10. **Get professional help.** You hire carpenters, roofers, plumbers, mechanics, doctors, and lawyers for their specialized expertise. Why wouldn't you do the same when fixing your financial health?

That's it in a nutshell. But I really wish you'd avoid the mistakes that many people make with their money —or at least stand up to the conventional muddled thinking that passes for wisdom. You can do that, too, ... if you keep reading.

■ HOW TO USE THIS BOOK

I've tried to make the book as easy to use as possible for you. As I wrote earlier, averages don't apply to you. Nothing fits everyone. Although this book addresses key principles that do apply to everyone, some of the specifics in these pages may not apply to you. Skip them. Pick the sections that apply to your situation—or your dreams.

Let me review quickly for you the key subjects I address in each chapter.

Chapter One is about the real purpose of financial planning: living your dream. What you want from life should dictate your financial plan and your strategies.

Chapter Two addresses the biggest mistake most people make in planning their financial future: they try to get lucky by picking one or two good investments, rather than developing a sound strategy first.

In Chapter Three I write about the myth of compounding interest. It's not a lie to say you can watch your money grow that way, but it's not a lie to say you can watch snails race, either. They move, just very slowly. More important to wealth enhancement is the acceleration of money.

Chapter Four is about debt and how you may be able to use debt to your advantage. But beware: most debt will destroy your chance of realizing your dreams.

Chapter Five attacks the myth of dollar-cost averaging as a way to invest, but the real subject is the danger of market timing. Now most experts will agree that market timing—trying to buy a stock, for instance, at its lowest price and sell it at its highest price—is a game that's nearly impossible to win. But some of those same gurus go on to encourage dollar-cost averaging, which is a poor person's market-timing strategy. They can't have it both ways.

Chapter Six will incur the wrath of a lot of financial advisers and institutions, maybe even your employer. I argue that pretax retirement plans are detrimental for many, maybe even most people. Your goal should be to enhance wealth, not just save some money.

Chapter Seven will be considered blasphemy by many, so get ready to be told that I'm an idiot. I take on all the people that tell you life insurance is not a good investment. It can be a very good investment, and I'll show you precisely why. And I'm not talking about term insurance; I mean the whole ball of wax—*permanent* life insurance. "Perm" should be a part of your financial future.

Chapter Eight seems terribly self-serving. I advise you to hire a financial planner, against the advice of many "experts" who seem to think it's too expensive. Your antennae should have just gone up. "Helmer's a financial planner," you should be thinking, "and he's going to make money if I follow his advice." That's right. But when I tell you why, I hope you'll see that it makes a lot of sense. I even tell you how to do it right.

Chapter Nine is a brief special chapter I've added for those people who want to consider good strategies for giving their money away—an increasing desire given the wealth that many have accumulated in recent years through stock market appreciation, inheritance, and the creation and growth of successful businesses. Due to tax laws, giving strategies take on a unique complexity that merit special attention in order to enhance the impact of gifts—and to generate important financial benefits to the person making the gift.

Chapter Ten was created to give you an easy and quick reference to the many types of investments you could make. I've not only provided a brief description, but also included my perspective on the advantages and disadvantages of each.

Chapter Eleven provides answers to questions I'm often asked. I hope those answers will illuminate some of the concepts I have discussed. I hope you will see topics that make sense to your specific needs and give you some useful ideas.

Chapter Twelve provides several profiles of hypothetical investors. While these are for illustrative purposes only, you may recognize in their situations some of the challenges you face.

Read, think, save, and invest. But most of all enjoy life. That's the only point of all the rest.

■ BE SURE TO READ THIS, TOO!

In various places in this book, I discuss and sometimes compare different investment products. Each of these products is designed to address certain investor needs and each has distinct risk and reward characteristics. Some of those differences are so marked that the regulators who supervise the securities industry require that financial professionals spell them out whenever we discuss these products—even in a book such as this, which does not purport to give advice about which products might be suitable for any specific individual.

With that said, here are some key facts about some of the investments I discuss in this book and about investments in general:

- Equity investments involve market risk, including fluctuating returns and possible loss of principal.
- Unlike equities, bonds offer a fixed interest rate and return of principal if held to maturity.
- High-yield bonds typically involve more risk of issuer default than investment-grade bonds.
- Government securities are backed by the full faith and credit of the United States.
- International investments involve special risks, including economic and political uncertainty and currency fluctuation.
- Small-capitalization stocks tend to experience greater volatility than large-capitalization stocks.
- Mutual funds and variable-rate contract investment sub-accounts involve fluctuating returns and values so that an investor's shares, when re-

deemed, may be worth more or less than their original cost. In addition, early withdrawals from and loans taken against variable-rate contracts may involve additional fees, tax penalties, and/ or negative effects on death benefits.

• Money market mutual funds are neither insured nor guaranteed by the U.S. Government and there can be no assurance that they will be able to maintain a stable net asset value of $1.00.

• Real estate and other sectoral investments may be subject to sectoral or regional economic downturns.

• Direct participation programs are generally illiquid and involve special risks. They may not be suitable for all investors.

• Unlike securities, CDs and other bank deposits offer a fixed interest rate and are FDIC-insured.

• The Dow Jones Industrial Average, the S & P 500, the Russell 5000, and other indexes are unmanaged. Investors cannot invest directly in indexes.

• Periodic investment plans do not assure a profit nor do they protect against losses in a declining market. Dollar-cost averaging involves continuous investment in securities regardless of the fluctuating price of such securities. Investors should carefully consider their financial ability to continue their investments during periods of low price levels.

• Past performance does not guarantee future results. The reason is simple, the markets will never be exactly the same again.

Throughout this book I use plenty of examples to illustrate financial concepts. These examples often employ hypothetical rates of return for different kinds of investments. In all cases, these rates of return are for illustration only and do not represent any specific investment.

DON'T AIM TOO LOW: PLAN TO GET WHAT YOU WANT

The Myth: In retirement you'll need about 70% of your working income.

The Reality: You may need 70% of your working income, but is that all you *want*?

Where do you begin? What's the point of planning, saving, and investing? If you begin where many industry experts and consultants advise, you may already be planning to fail. Don't start with *needs* planning. Needs planning is very popular and is the prevalent planning methodology in the financial industry today. It's one of the worst things you could do—and indicates a financial outlook that I constantly fight. If you base your planning on what you need, you're aiming too low. In the 1970s the Rolling Stones sang, "You can't always get what you want..." —but why would anyone plan for anything less?

■ THE EEYORE SCHOOL OF FINANCIAL PLANNING

If you don't have young kids around, you may have forgotten about Eeyore, the donkey in the wonderful Winnie the Pooh books. Eeyore walks around with a cloud over his head; he's always pessimistic. Eeyore's philosophy of life is, "If something can go wrong, it probably will." The world is full of needs planners and their alma mater was the Eeyore School of Financial Planning.

Here's how needs planning works: You decide that it's time to plan for your retirement. You make $50,000 a year working and, following traditional financial thinking, decide that you need 70% of that income for retirement. Therefore, instead of $50,000, you plan to make $35,000. Now that's a "Gloomy Place," as Eeyore's meadow is called.

At retirement your cost of living may be lower than ever, but isn't that the time to enjoy the fruits of your years of labor? How much fun can you have on $35,000 per year? My point is this: you may need only $35,000 per year, but how much do you want? Your financial plan should be designed to help you get what you want, not just what you need.

Why limit yourself to your perceived need rather than realizing your full financial potential? You should attempt to determine accurately your need, then exceed it. If you're embarking on a 100-mile car trip and your car gets 20 miles per gallon, you need five gallons of gas in your tank. My advice to you, however, would be to fill your tank before you leave. What if you encounter a traffic jam, a detour, or bad weather?

Needs planning is based on several assumptions that you are average—and we've already established that you're not and don't want to be.

False Assumption #1: You'll Spend Less on Discretionary Items in Retirement

---

How exactly will you spend less in retirement? Maybe you will if you're happy to sit at home year round and read books borrowed from the library. Most people, however, have big plans for retirement—the first time in their adult lives that they can do precisely what they want to do. They plan to travel, play golf whenever they feel like it, pursue their hobbies. But all of those activities require money—probably more money than you'll save by not having work-related expenses.

Even social life changes for many people when they retire. The social aspect of work is lost; the camaraderie of the work place is gone. To make up for it, people go out with friends more often. But where do they go? They meet for lunch or dinner—and probably spend more on dining in retirement than ever before.

Many people assume as well that they'll spend less on possessions. After all, don't they already own the furniture, the TV, all their kitchen appliances? True, but what of the next generation of technological advances? Will you buy a computer? Maybe you already have one, but will you want to upgrade it so you can watch movies on it—any movie, any time—and use it as a videophone to talk to and watch your grandchildren? Or will you be content to stick with older technology and just replace your old VCR with a new DVD player?

Technology advancements and planned obsolescence will certainly continue to change everyone's lives. Think of our many "necessities" today that were luxuries yesterday. When did telephones become a necessity? When will portable or cellular phones be viewed the same as old rotary telephones once were? What will the next 10 or 20 years bring? What new conveniences will become commonplace? Will you keep up to date? Will it matter? To most people it will—and they will buy the new conveniences. That takes money.

Before you plan to retire on an income based on a needs-planning target of 70% of your income, I challenge you to do some calculating. If you're making $50,000 now, as in our example above, and plan to retire on $35,000, figure out how you're going to spend $15,000 less every year. Your Golden Ager's discount at movie theaters isn't going to cut your cost of living by 30%—not unless you see a lot of movies, in which case I recommend that you replace your old VCR immediately.

False Assumption #2: Your Housing Costs Will Be Much Lower in Retirement

---

If your mortgage is paid off, your housing costs could drop significantly. That will be true for many people who have lived in the same house for the last three decades and paid for it—which is not many people in this day and age. But even that is no guarantee that your costs are going to plummet. I know of people who have had to sell their homes because their retirement income wasn't high enough to pay the property taxes. They had the "misfortune" of owning a home in a desirable neighborhood where property values skyrocketed and their property taxes followed. Of course they made some money by selling their houses, but they loved their homes and their neighborhoods—it was painful to leave.

■ WANTS PLANNING: REALIZE YOUR POTENTIAL!

Needs planning is great advice for the masses—those who aren't planning at all now and need some place to start. It's a great way to convince people that they should save something, but it's pitiful advice for people who want to do better than get by. Don't settle for mediocrity in your investment planning. Try to excel. It's fine to set a floor or a minimum for what you'll need to get by, but then aim a little higher—and plan to get there! Become a "wants" planner.

Many of my clients retire with higher annual incomes than when they were working. My own personal plan is designed to exceed my average annual working income. Don't be satisfied to

be one of the "70%ers"—people striving, to use the word lightly, to retire at 70% of their working income just because they've been brainwashed to believe that's what they'll need.

■ WHAT DO YOU WANT?

Instead of planning to meet your needs based on some percentage of your working income, ask yourself what you want from life. What life have you imagined? What is your dream? Few people hesitate when asked about their dream. For some the dream is a secure retirement, perhaps early, with the time, comfort, and good health to enjoy family and friends. Others imagine the opportunity to pursue passions: art, music, travel, perhaps even the infuriating white dimpled ball or the wily walleye. Perhaps you dream of education and security for your children or grandchildren, leaving a legacy in your community, or improving life for future generations. Your financial plan begins with your dreams, because they are the true currency of your life.

Each reader will have different objectives or dreams, but you will probably fall into one of four basic categories.

1. Money to live. You want to create wealth to give you the wherewithal to live the way you want to. You probably don't need to wallow in luxury; most of us don't. But you'd like the freedom to spend a few extra dollars here or there. Some people want to live better through possessions— nicer furniture, a better car, a few classy additions to the wardrobe,

a house in a different neighborhood, a second home or cabin in the mountains, at the beach, or on a lake. But many people don't value "things." Many of you want to live better through experiences: a week or two in Provence; a hike along the Great Wall of China; a chance to follow in the footsteps of Lewis and Clark from the Mississippi to the Pacific; a season subscription to a favorite opera company, symphony orchestra, or baseball team; a week with your grandchildren at Disney World; or just a quiet meal in an elegant restaurant once in a while. You want wealth so you can spend it on possessions or experiences—whether your desires are modest or grand.

2. Money to save. Your primary financial goal is simply to be free from worry about money. To you it's not so important what you can do with the wealth you create, but what you can't do—relax—without it. You want to have enough so that maybe for the first time in your life you aren't afraid that you'll have to replace the aging shingles on your roof or the noisy clothes washer in your basement. Being in this category is not just a matter of having or not having a lot of money now. Some people, no matter how much they have, worry that it's not enough. I don't get into psychological diagnoses, but childhood experiences have a lot to do with how people answer the question, "How much is enough?"

3. Money to give. You want to accumulate wealth so you can give it away. The causes that may motivate you are as different and varied as the flavors at your local ice cream parlor. I have advised many people who want to be able to make greater contributions to their churches or alma maters. Others dream of supporting an artistic organization with their money, believing that the arts not only enrich their own lives, but enlighten the world.

4. Money to pass down. If you fall into this category, one of your primary objectives is to leave a bequest to children or grandchildren. In this category, too, motivations may vary greatly among individuals. Perhaps you want your children and their children to have opportunities you never had. Maybe you want to ensure that they have enough to get by, because they certainly don't have your nose for making money. Or maybe you have to look after them because your daughter married some idle dreamer of a ne'er-do-well whom you don't trust to provide for your grandchildren.

You probably see a little of yourself in each of the four descriptions. Most people dream of a combination of these lives; they want a little of each. But when I first meet with prospective clients, I always ask them about their dream, and most are fairly specific— one of these objectives stands out above the others.

My point in raising the issue of dreams is that each of these objectives suggests a different approach—a different strategy for creating wealth. So your strategy should begin with your dreams. Before you even open the stock market pages of your newspaper or log onto the Internet to research stocks, take out a piece of paper and write in a single sentence or two what your dream is. Ask yourself, "Why do I want to create wealth? What will it mean to me?"

■ CONCLUSION

The greatest limitations on most of us are self-imposed—and needs planners encourage self-limiting behavior. When you are beginning to plan your financial future, why place such constraints on yourself? Create a financial road map to get you to the destination you really want to reach, not halfway there. Don't worry now about whether your goals are realistic. When I ask clients what they want, I very rarely hear goals that are absurdly unrealistic in terms of their net worth or income. And a good

number of my clients that have set "ambitious" goals have reached them. I don't think they would have done as well if they had been content just to plan for their needs.

My concern isn't that you will want something unattainable; it's that you won't plan to achieve what you really want. Don't let anyone tell you what you will need. Be clear in your own mind what you really want. Then plan to get it.

■ HELMER'S HINTS

- Don't accept the artificial constraints of conventional wisdom. Think, plan, and dream for yourself.

- Only with a clear goal in mind— your dream for your life—can you plan effectively. Amassing money isn't much of a goal in itself. The wealthier people that I have advised, without exception, have had some dream beyond adding zeros to their net worth. At its best, financial planning provides not only a course of action, but also motivation for achieving what you want out of life.

GET A GRIP: PICKING STOCKS WON'T MAKE YOU WEALTHY

The Myth: Getting rich depends on buying the right stocks.

The Reality: An investment strategy is far more important.

Traditional financial thinking emphasizes where you put your money, which investment vehicle—or stock—you should pick. The far more important issue is *how* your money should be invested.

To use a golf analogy: if you are an extremely poor golfer, would you attempt to improve your game by buying an expensive new set of clubs or would you take lessons to improve your stance, grip, and swing?

Obviously, lessons would do more to improve your game than new clubs. In fact, new clubs probably won't help your game at all if your golfing mechanics are wrong. That said, I know more golfers who regularly buy new clubs than take lessons—and they still struggle to break into double figures. I also know more investors who study stock reports than plan an investment strategy—and wonder why they can't equal, let alone beat, market averages.

Prevailing wisdom is selling consumers new sets of clubs. "Sell mutual fund ABC and buy fund XYZ!" "Get rid of your small-cap stocks; large caps is the place to be." "You need more equities! Or is it fewer equities?" "The Dow will crash." "The Dow will soar." And so on.

You should be looking for a lesson on improving the efficiency of your mechanics. Leave the new clubs to those who have such beautiful swings that they can take advantage of minor improvements in golf club technology.

With investing, these improvements can create additional capital to invest. If you can have more money without detracting from your current lifestyle, you eliminate one of the primary reasons most people do not save or invest. You now have created more wealth—and investment vehicles matter even less. Strategies can create investment dollars.

■ BEYOND YOUR WILDEST DREAMS

You've already defined your dream. You know what you want from life and how money can help you get it. Now how do you get there? What is your strategy?

To create an effective strategy for realizing your dream, you have to consider three central questions. (And remember: you are still a long way from picking stocks for your portfolio!)

A good financial strategy is based on answers to three critical questions:

1. What type of money are you investing?
2. What impact will taxes have on your investments?
3. How will you manage your investments?

■ WHAT TYPE OF MONEY ARE YOU INVESTING?

When I talk about type of money, it's not cash, check, or plastic. From a financial planning standpoint, there are actually five different types of money or investable capital: *new money, old money, old money earnings, additional money, and strategy-created money.*

1. **New money.** New money is discretionary capital that remains after you've fulfilled all of your economic obligations and lifestyle costs. In other words, you receive a paycheck, then use that check to pay your bills, go out for dinner with your spouse, and buy a new weed whacker. Anything that remains for you to invest would be new money. If you selected an investment that depreciates in value, you would actually be losing your hard-earned dollars. Consequently, from a planning standpoint, you may want to take a conservative approach when you invest new money.

2. **Old money.** Old money can be defined as the money that you've already invested. It may be money in your savings account,

your CDs, your mutual funds, your 401(k) account, and other investments.

3. **Old money earnings.** It just makes sense that the interest or return on your old money is "old money earnings." For example, if your $10,000 of old money is in a CD earning 5%, the CD will generate $500 of old money earnings in a year. The American public has been taught that old money earnings should compound or accumulate within that specific investment. In other words, your old money will continue to get bigger and bigger. As I demonstrate in Chapter 3, this is a huge strategic mistake.

4. **Additional money.** Any unexpected source of investable capital is additional money—a windfall. It is not consistent or predictable. An accident settlement, a tax refund, a bonus, or gambling winnings would all be defined as additional money. Since this windfall is typically seen as extra money, you may want to be particularly aggressive with it.

5. **Strategy-created money.** As you'd guess, strategy-created money is any investable capital that exists due to a financial planning strategy. This newly created capital could come about in many ways. A strategy that reduces your income taxes allows you to invest the tax savings, which otherwise would earn no

return. You can also create investable capital if you use strategic planning to consolidate your debts and free up dollars that previously went to service the debt. This money that you create can be invested aggressively. Even if the investment depreciates in value, you haven't really lost anything because the dollars didn't exist previously.

We know we need to save or invest, but we're reluctant to do it because we must make some sacrifices to do so. It's comparable to getting into better physical shape. We know we need to exercise, eat fruit and vegetables, drink plenty of water, and eat foods high in fiber and low in fat, yet it's difficult to do these things. It's difficult because we have to sacrifice—just as we must sacrifice for proper saving and investing. But if a planning strategy creates a dollar of investable capital, it's easy to invest that dollar because you don't have to detract from your lifestyle in order to do it. In other words, no sacrifice is *necessary*. Strategy-created money is one of the most important benefits of efficient financial planning.

■ WHAT IS THE IMPACT OF TAXES ON YOUR INVESTMENTS?

In the effort to enhance your wealth, you have to consider the impact of taxes on your financial future. Until and unless our tax structure changes, they must be a consideration in any investment strategy.

How should you look at taxes in your financial strategy? This is the second big question in determining an investment strategy. Tax reduction strategies give almost everyone the opportunity to create investable capital. But the strategy has to go beyond what you've probably considered in the past. The more investable money you have, of course, the more you can take advantage of tax reduction strategies. But nearly everyone can do something to create investable money by reducing taxes.

Don't for a minute assume that you have to bend the law or break it to reduce your taxes. The U.S. Congress has created widely accepted, if too little used, ways to reduce taxes. As we will see in a moment, our government has used tax credits and deductions to motivate individuals to address specific problems in our society.

The impact of taxes is too often ignored when considering investment strategies. Maybe you've heard the advice that you should consider investments on their own merit—setting aside the tax consequences. *While that advice doesn't quite rise to the level of dangerous myth, it's still horrible advice.* If you ever hear it, cover your ears and run away as fast as you can because someone is probably trying to sell you something you don't want.

That's a little bit like telling you that you shouldn't concern yourself with the rate of return on your investment. Which investment would look better to you, one that earned 10% or one that earned 7%? It's a no-brainer. If your federal tax rate is 31%, a taxable investment at 10% is really paying only 6.9% after taxes. Of course, taxes matter! If you compare two investments that will be taxed the same, then it's not an issue. But here's a thought: why not look for investments that will pay you the highest rate of return *after* taxes?

(I won't address the issue of estate taxes. While that's an important issue for many of my clients, it affects only about 2% of the population. If you'd like to learn more about estate planning, I'd recommend that you read *A Practical Guide to Successful Estate Planning*, a book recently co-written by my associate Tom Petracek.)

■ THREE FILE CABINETS

From a tax perspective, we have three investment possibilities, three options that I look at as three file cabinets. A good financial plan will use all three— although the ideal investment products in your three cabinets may be different from your brother's, for instance.

1. **Taxable Investments.** The first file cabinet would contain all of your taxable investments. We won't distinguish here between money that's treated as ordinary income and capital gains. Taxable investments include money-market accounts, CDs, mutual funds, stocks and bonds, and everything else that's treated as a loss or gain fully and immediately when it is credited. All of these types of investments give you almost immediate access to your money when you need it.

I recommend trying to have enough money in liquid accounts to cover living expenses for three months. When I say liquid accounts, I'm not suggesting that you buy stock in Coca-Cola or Budweiser. Liquid assets are assets that can be converted into cash (liquidated) quickly at any time. A checking account is very liquid; a Stradivarius violin or a 1952 Mickey Mantle baseball card is not. The violin and the card may be worth far more than your checking account, but you couldn't just sell them on the street corner. You'd have to find a qualified buyer, which could take some time, and the buyer would have to meet your price. If you were forced to unload your fiddle or Mickey quickly, you might have to sell at a substantial loss or at least at a price well below the current market value.

Occasionally you'll hear someone talk about having a "liquidity" problem. That could mean the person is worth billions, but those billions are all tied up in investments that can't be liquidated easily. (It could also mean that a person is flat broke and is putting it in the best light!) You can avoid the worst liquidity problems by maintaining some investments in this first file cabinet.

2. **Tax-Deferred Investments.** The second file cabinet is for tax-deferred investments. This would include any non-qualified tax-deferred annuity, individual retirement account (IRA), simplified employee pension, 401(k),

403(b), Keogh, 457, or any other pretax retirement plans where the amount of the contribution is deducted from your income for tax purposes in the year in which you make the contribution. Most investors put the lion's share of their investment dollars into this file cabinet. As we'll see in Chapter 6, over-funding these types of investments can actually be inefficient and counterproductive.

3. **Tax-Advantaged Investments.** The third file cabinet is for tax-advantaged investments. An ideal financial plan has dollars in all three file cabinets. Unfortunately, most investors have the tax-deferred file cabinet overflowing and do not even have a third file cabinet. Tax-advantaged investments would include those that are tax-free or tax-deductible or that give the investor a tax credit. The essential difference between this file cabinet and the second one is that tax-advantaged investments aren't just taxed at a later time; all or part of the earnings from a tax-advantaged investment aren't taxed at all. Obviously, all things being equal, tax-free is preferable to taxable or tax-deferred.

Let's look briefly at each—because you can actually use these investments to reduce taxes and create investable capital.

TAX-FREE INVESTMENT STRATEGIES

You have only three options for investment earnings that are potentially free of income tax: municipal bonds or municipal bond funds, life insurance, and (since 1998) a Roth IRA. Each is described in Chapter 10.

TAX-DEDUCTIBLE INVESTMENT STRATEGIES

The most common tax deduction is interest on home mortgage payments. However, very few investors realize that certain investment strategies may also generate tax deductions. Other deductions work the same as the mortgage deduction: you would subtract them from your income before you calculate your tax.

ENERGY INVESTMENTS

Energy investments, usually in oil and gas drilling ventures, are an efficient way to invest and achieve tax deductions. The reason for the tax deduction on energy investments can be traced to our country's reluctance to be dependent on foreign energy sources. The tax deduction is an incentive to private investors to attempt to enhance and improve this country's ability to develop our own energy resources.

A high-quality energy strategy could allow for a tax deduction exceeding 90%. So, if you were to invest $100,000, the tax deduction would be $90,000. The tax deduction—in this case $90,000—is multiplied by the investor's tax bracket. Assuming a 36% tax bracket, the investor in this example would have actual tax savings of $32,400. The investor has the potential gains accruing to an investment of $100,000, yet has really invested only $67,600, because a partner has invested $32,400. Who's that partner? Uncle Sam!

Generally, these programs are most attractive to investors in moderately high tax brackets. They may not be suitable for all investors for a number of reasons. For example, these programs may involve considerable risk and they are generally illiquid. The second point is especially important to bear in mind if you believe you might need the money before the program expires.

Also, obviously, the underlying investment must have an opportunity for gain or this would not be a smart strategy. It would be counterproductive to spend $100,000 to save $32,400. Unless the underlying investment earns a profit, the net result would be a $67,600 loss.

Energy investments are usually set up as limited partnerships—a term that makes some people cringe because they've had negative experiences with them. But I like to use the analogy of a car to represent the limited partnership. Now the car could be driven by an odious felon or by the Pope—and driven for many purposes. The key question is, "Who's driving the car?" I suspect that many more people have been ripped off, and for a lot more money, by dishonest general partners creating fraudulent limited partnerships than by street muggers. But in the right hands, limited partnerships have the potential to be a very powerful investment tool. In certain aspects they are similar to mutual funds: many people put their money in the hands of a manager to achieve a specific purpose and then they share the returns in proportion to their investment. You just have to be sure you know something about the person driving the car—the general partner. (Also, as noted, limited partnerships are almost always highly illiquid, while mutual funds can be sold at any time.)

Let's see how the tax-deductible strategy could work. Assume you sell a highly appreciated asset—meaning that it's worth a lot more now than when you bought it. If you sell stock for $100,000 that cost you $37,000, you have a $63,000 gain. The tax liability on the gain (assuming a 20% capital gains tax rate and excluding state taxes) would be approximately $12,600. If you applied $50,000 to an energy investment with a 90% tax deduction, you would offset the entire tax liability from selling the stock. (See Figure 2.1.) Furthermore, you actually could implement the energy strategy December 31 and receive the tax deduction for the entire preceding calendar year. This is potentially a very attractive strategy.

Tax Deductible Investment Strategy: Energy Investment

Stock sale price	$100,000	Energy investment	$ 50,000
Stock purchase price	– 37,000	Tax deduction (90%)	x .90
Gain	$ 63,000	Allowable deduction	$ 45,000
Capital gains tax (20%)	x .20	Federal tax rate (28%)	x .28
Federal tax due	$ 12,600	Federal tax deduction	$ 12,600

Figure 2.1

In this example, you could balance the capital gains taxes on the sale of stock by investing half of the proceeds in an energy investment. And you still have $50,000 in proceeds from the stock sale and the potential earnings from your energy investment.

TAX CREDITS

Unlike tax deductions, which are subtracted from income before calculating tax, tax credits are subtracted directly from what you owe in taxes. Tax credits are a dollar-for-dollar forgiveness of your bottom-line tax liability—which makes them even more valuable than tax deductions. If your tax liability were $10,000 and you used a strategy to generate $3,000 in credits, your new tax liability would only be $7,000.

HOUSING INVESTMENTS

An efficient method of generating tax credits is through affordable housing investments. These investments resemble mutual funds in that a manager "pools" all the investors' money. However, rather than acquire stock, the manager acquires or develops housing that meets federal government standards as "affordable." (Keep in mind that, unlike mutual funds, these investments are generally illiquid.)

The government established tax credits for developing affordable housing to encourage investors to address a serious shortage of affordable housing in the United States, a shortage that may become more acute as more baby boomers retire and live on fixed incomes. (These are the "average" folks who accept as wisdom the myths I'm discussing and don't plan like you will!) Rather than appropriate money to develop the housing that's needed, the government provides incentives for the private sector to develop affordable housing by offering tax credits to investors.

A quality affordable housing tax credit program pays $1.15 to $1.20 for every $1.00 invested. Therefore, a $10,000 investment would generate $11,500 to $12,000 in tax credits. These credits are generally delivered over a 10-year period of time. Consequently, the investor would save $1,150 to $1,200 in taxes per year for 10 years.

One of the more attractive features of tax credit investment strategies is the potential opportunity gain. In other words, the money being saved in taxes is strategy-created capital that can now be invested elsewhere. The ability to apply earnings to previously unavailable investable capital can significantly enhance the overall performance of a portfolio.

Fast-forward into the future and imagine retiring. To supplement your retirement income, you plan to withdraw $25,000 per year from your IRA. In a 28% federal tax bracket, the

Once again, you have to exercise prudence in your selection of partners in housing investments. And just as you never want to invest without considering the tax implications, you never want to invest for only tax reasons. Always look at the potential return on your investment. Tax reduction is simply one part of the potential return that must be analyzed. If, in the previous example, you withdrew the $60,000 from an investment that was earning a hypothetical return of 20% a year,

Tax Credit Strategy: Affordable Housing Investment

IRA withdrawal		$ 25,000	Affordable housing investment	$ 60,000
Federal tax rate (28%)	x	.28	Tax credit/year (11.67%)	x .1167
Tax due		$ 7,000	Tax credit	$ 7,000

Figure 2.2

$25,000 withdrawal would trigger $7,000 of additional tax.

Independently of the IRA, you also have a portfolio of taxable investments. Remember that you want some of your money in each of the three file cabinets. Repositioning $60,000 of that portfolio into an affordable housing tax credit strategy should generate about $7,000 in tax savings—which effectively cancels the tax on your IRA distribution. Therefore, the net result is that you essentially withdraw $25,000 tax-free from your IRA! Most affordable housing tax credit programs generate credits for 10 years. Consequently, you could withdraw $250,000 from your IRA with *no net tax liability*! (See Figure 2.2.)

you'd be losing money after taxes by shifting it into the housing investment.

Both of the tax-advantaged investment strategies I've discussed—housing and energy—are likely to be available for some time, because the shortage of affordable housing and domestic energy sources is not likely to be corrected any time soon.

■ HOW WILL YOU MANAGE YOUR INVESTMENTS?

As we've looked at what you should consider in creating an effective financial and investment strategy, I've encouraged you to answer two questions, so far: "What type of money will

I invest?" and "What are the tax implications of my strategy?" The third question you have to ask is "How will I manage my investments?"

If your answer is that you will manage your investments yourself, that's fine—but be prepared to spend a lot of time and energy. Managing your investments effectively is far more important and difficult than most people realize. Remember: it's not about just picking stocks. (See Chapter 8 for more advice on how to choose a financial planner to advise you and how to work with that planner or, if you think you're up to it, how to create a sound financial plan yourself.)

I think you'll have a better idea why it's so important and so difficult if we take a closer look at the keys to sound investing on a strategic level. There are two: asset allocation and continuous portfolio management.

■ ASSET ALLOCATION: PEPSI OR COKE?

Asset allocation simply means which types of investments you choose. You allocate assets every time you go to the store. The last time I stopped at a convenience store I allocated $15.29 for gas, $2.98 for Diet Pepsi, and $3.19 for Doritos.

When we allocate assets for investment purposes, we're usually talking about asset classes—or types of assets. If I looked at the things I bought at the convenience store that way, I could say that I'd allocated $15.29 for Fuel, $2.98 for Drink, and $3.19 for Food. Why? Because if I were tracking my spending

and sticking to a budget, it wouldn't matter if I had spent the $2.98 on Pepsi or Coke.

Asset allocation in investment terms uses a similar logic. It groups similar types of investments into categories. In fact, investments are usually considered to fall into one of 21 widely accepted asset classes.

Let's take a moment to explain a few basic investment terms. (See Chapter 10 for some of the key differences between these asset classes.)

"Cap" is an abbreviation of capitalization, meaning the market value of a company's total outstanding stock (share price x shares outstanding).

- Large Cap: More than $5 billion
- Mid Cap: $1-5 billion
- Small Cap: $100 million - $1 billion
- Micro Cap: Less than $100 million.

A company with 100 million shares of stock issued with a market price of $100 a share is a large-cap company. A company with 2 million shares of issued stock with a market price of $20 a share is a micro-cap company.

The terms "growth" and "value" are used to define the focus of investors or mutual fund managers. Growth investors are looking primarily at how fast a company is growing. These investors would buy shares in a rapidly growing company even if the shares were relatively high-priced. Value investors are looking primarily for stocks that are cheap, or undervalued, in comparison with what they believe

Asset Classes

- Cash (or short-term obligations such as a 3-month Treasury Bill)
- Real Estate (investments are often made through a real estate investment trust [REIT], which works like a mutual fund)
- Commodities (metals, agricultural products)
- Bonds
- Short-Term Government Bonds (1- to 3-year maturity)
- Intermediate-Term Government Bonds (5-10 years)
- Long-Term Government Bonds (30 years)
- Corporate Bonds
- Municipal Bonds
- High-Yield Bonds
- International Bonds
- Emerging Market Bonds
- Stocks
- Large-Cap Value Stocks
- Large-Cap Growth Stocks
- Mid-Cap Stocks
- Small-Cap Value Stocks
- Small-Cap Growth Stocks
- Micro-Cap Stocks
- Actively Managed Large-Cap Stocks
- International Stocks
- Emerging Market Stocks
- Low-Turnover Stocks (usually an index of stocks, such as the S&P 500)

Figure 2.3

the underlying assets are worth or with other companies in the same industry.

Asset allocation has been the subject of extensive study by economists and investors, but the critical importance of asset allocation really came to the fore with the work of Harry Markowitz, William Sharpe, and Merton Miller, three economists who won the 1990 Nobel Prize in Economics for creating *modern portfolio theory*.

Here's their conclusion in a nutshell: sound asset allocation has the potential to simultaneously enhance expected performance and reduce risk. Please note that I did not say that asset allocation only reduces risk, but that it also has the potential to enhance return. Moreover, they concluded that asset allocation is *the* dominant factor in determining total portfolio return.

They demonstrated that the performance of an investment portfolio depends mostly—over 90%—on the asset classes in which that portfolio was invested. The other two factors the professors considered—stock selection and market timing—had minimal effects on performance. In their study, the overwhelming determinant of the successful investment strategy was not which securities or mutual funds were bought or sold, but how assets were divided among the various asset classes.

You see, when I said that picking stocks won't necessarily make you wealthy, I knew I had the backing of Nobel Prize-winning economists—even though your Uncle Wilbur may not agree with them. The professors further demonstrated that for every level of risk there is some optimum combination of asset classes that will provide the highest rate of return.

■ THE ASSET ALLOCATION HOUSE

A portfolio isn't just a collection of assets, any more than a house is just a collection of rooms. If you own a bunch of assets without proper asset allocation, you may have a house with two dining rooms, four living rooms, but no bathrooms or kitchen. Proper asset allocation, on the other hand, is

like saying, "I need a house with four bedrooms, one big kitchen, three baths, a living room, and a family room, and here's how big I'd like them each to be." Now you've got a functional house—a house that meets your specific needs. What you've done is allocated space. Well, a portfolio is your allocation of investment space. Instead of doing it by rooms or square footage, you do it by percentages of your resources in asset classes: 50% in this type of asset, 40% in that, 10% in another.

Modern portfolio theory demonstrates that a proper mix of assets provides an optimal combination of risk and return. And when planning your life, your future, you have to think of risk and return in their broadest terms. Risk may not mean losing money; it may mean losing opportunities—in financial or personal terms. Reward may be more than making more money; it may mean increasing financial security or enhancing your enjoyment of life. The goal is to earn a solid return over an extended period of time in a variety of unpredictable market conditions, rather than chase the highest possible return at any one given point in time.

Only after you have determined a strategy and allocated space in your portfolio is it time to consider the merits of specific products. Buying those products is like putting the furniture in each room of your investment house.

Maybe you want a big old overstuffed easy chair in your living room, very comfortable—similar to an annuity or insurance that provides security. Maybe you want an entertainment wall in your family room, with all the latest electronic gadgets—like high-flying equities. Maybe you want to make room in your study for the big oak desk you inherited from your grandfather—like a trust for the education of your grandchildren.

The options are practically endless. The first requirement is that the furniture fit in the rooms of your house—the asset classes in your portfolio—that's located in the neighborhood or in the city or in the state that offers everything you've ever wanted—your strategy.

To access the full return potential of the financial markets and help reduce risk, portfolios must be diversified within each asset class as well. The stock and bond markets are composed of numerous styles and sectors (large value, small growth, international equities, government bonds, corporate bonds, etc.). A prudent management philosophy will have carefully designed strategies for the domestic equity market, international equity market, fixed income market, and so on.

To conclude the asset allocation house analogy, I want you to remember one thing above all else. I call it the "investing corollary of the real estate rule." What are the three most important things to remember about investing? Allocation, allocation, allocation.

■ NEGATIVE CORRELATION IS POSITIVE

It's easy to allocate space in a house based on the size of your family, your needs, and your lifestyle. But how do you decide to allocate space in your investment house? Investment professionals look at three basic components of each asset class: expected rate of return, expected risk level, and expected correlation with other asset classes. It is important to note that "expected" does not mean "guaranteed." Professionals study historical performance knowing full well that it does not guarantee future results.

- **Expected rate of return** is simply a historical calculation: how the asset class has performed on average over an extended period of time.

- **Expected risk level** is a mathematical calculation of the historical average variance from the historical expected rate of return. The greater the average variance, the greater the likelihood that performance has been significantly different from the expected rate of return in any given year.

- **Expected correlation with other asset classes** is determined by comparing historical performance for various asset classes. Over time, we learn that some asset classes tend to perform similarly or quite the opposite of other asset classes.

If we fill our portfolio with only asset classes that tend to perform alike, we may very well increase our risk. If market and economic conditions favor those asset classes, we could do very well. But if any of those asset classes performs badly, they probably will all go into the tank. Our other option, a much smarter option, is to balance asset classes: in other words, find the optimum combination of asset classes to enhance performance and reduce overall portfolio volatility.

Even if one asset class tends to be very risky, meaning that it can fluctuate wildly over time, we try to balance that asset class with another that also appears risky but tends to move in the opposite direction. Our objective is to reduce the risk in our portfolio and increase the returns over time. That's an example of negative correlation— which is positive in asset allocation.

■ THE SUNNY SHORES OF RAINY LAKE

To put negative correlation in simple terms, consider this love story. A young woman opened a resort on beautiful Rainy Lake in northern Minnesota. She was a very smart businessperson and her guests adored her. Her problem was that her business was very much dependent on the weather. In a hot, sunny summer, she made a 50% return on her investment. But in cold, damp summers, she would typically lose 25%. The ups and downs were a little unsettling for her.

But as luck would have it, one of her regular guests was a bachelor who

Sample Asset Class Performance 1990-1998*

Index	Standard & Poor's 500	Lehman Brothers Corporate/ Government bonds	MSCI Europe, Asia & Far East	Wilshire REIT	Muldex Very Small Cap
1990	-3.12	9.17	-23.45	-23.44	-16.02
1991	30.48	14.63	12.13	23.84	62.96
1992	7.62	7.17	-12.17	15.28	9.21
1993	10.06	8.78	32.56	15.46	12.42
1994	1.32	-1.93	7.78	0.79	4.59
1995	37.53	15.31	11.21	12.24	44.23
1996	22.95	4.06	6.05	37.08	11.71
1997	33.35	7.87	1.78	19.54	8.72
1998	28.58	8.42	20.00	-16.96	-1.92

Each of the five asset classes selected shows a loss in at least one year, but in no year did they all show losses.

*Source: *Stocks, Bonds, Bills and Inflation*® *2000 Yearbook,* ©2000 Ibbotson Associates, Inc. Based on copyrighted works by Ibbotson and Sinquefield. All rights reserved. Used with permission.

Figure 2.4

owned an umbrella company. His business had the opposite problem: in clear, sunny weather, his business lost 25%, but when the weather was blustery and wet, he enjoyed a hefty 50% return on his investment.

Perhaps it was inevitable that the resort owner and the umbrella maker fell in love, got married, and pooled their assets. Now neither of them worries about the weather because, rain or shine, they make a nice, steady 12.5% on their combined investment.

That's negative correlation—and that's the objective of asset allocation as well as diversification within a portfolio. This is clearly an oversimplification to make a point, but the goal of money management philosophy should be very simple. With a well-diversified, actively managed portfolio we attempt to achieve competitive long-term performance with less exposure to risk.

Of course, if the resort owner and umbrella maker were extremely good at guessing which summers would be sunny and which would be rainy, they could take full advantage of both conditions, shifting their assets as appropriate, and really make a killing. But anyone who could predict whether a summer will be bright and warm or cold and damp would have a gift that they could use to such financial advantage that they wouldn't need advice from me on how to create wealth.

Guessing the ups and downs of the stock market is not unlike anticipating the weather well in advance. Not even the professionals are right all the time—in weather or stocks—and they're smart enough to know it. So they try to reduce their risk and increase the potential for return by using percentages. The meteorologist says we have a 60% chance of rain. The money manager says we have 60% of our portfolio in stocks, 30% in bonds, and 10% in cash.

Your individual circumstances will determine how you should allocate your assets. People with a longer time horizon, such as someone who is only 30 years old, are probably best off fully invested in equities. Over the length of time that they are likely to be invested, stocks will almost certainly outperform all other asset classes. As people get older, their asset allocation should weigh two factors: their dependence on income from their investments and the amount of debt they have. Those who have higher net worth and low or no debt will likely want to remain fully invested in stocks or maintain a high percentage of their portfolio in equities.

■ CONTINUOUS PORTFOLIO MANAGEMENT: YOUR SECURITY SYSTEM

OK, you've built your dream home and stocked it with furniture that you love, furniture that's suited to your taste and your lifestyle. What's the next logical step for most people? Insurance and a security system.

Insurance and a security system for your home essentially do the same thing: protect your possessions. They both provide some security that you won't lose what you have—and you're willing to pay for them.

Portfolio management is very similar to your home security system. You've created your strategy, allocated space to asset classes, and then selected investment products in those classes. Portfolio management now protects your investments—which probably have a greater value than the possessions in your house. Let's put the question this way: "Which would you rather lose, your investments and life savings or your sofa?" If you lose your sofa, you can replace it from your investments. If you lose your investments—well, you can always lie down on your sofa for a good cry.

■ DON'T LOSE YOUR BALANCE

Unfortunately, once you've allocated assets, your work isn't over. Portfolio management is the ongoing confirmation and monitoring of your strategy: it must be continuous. Your situation will change, markets will change, and even your dreams may change. Your portfolio has to adjust, regardless of where the change originates. You have to continuously reassess your life, your goals, your portfolio, and your returns to ensure that you keep a mix of assets designed to achieve your goals. You have to rebalance your portfolio regularly.

You've probably seen gymnasts compete on the balance beam in the Olympics. The difference between those who win medals and those who don't is often just little adjustments in balance—a slight lean, a movement of the arms to compensate in one direction or the other. Occasionally the adjustment isn't enough and, to gasps from the announcers and crowd, the gymnast falls off the four-inch-wide beam. Rebalancing your portfolio isn't much different from making those shifts in the center of gravity that determine whether the gymnast falls or wins the gold.

Let's provide a theoretical example to demonstrate the principle of rebalancing your portfolio—keeping in mind that theories, like financial and investment myths, assume an average market and the markets, like you, aren't average at any given moment.

In the first year, you invest $10,000 in each of two hypothetical mutual funds. Fund ABC loses 50% of its value. Fund XYZ appreciates 100%. So now you have $25,000, a good performance for a year. But now you face a choice: whether or not to do anything with those funds.

Let's examine three strategies.

Strategy #1: None (buy and hold is barely a strategy). Let's say that you decide to take no action, that your strategy is to "buy and hold"—a strategy recommended by many financial planners and investment gurus. (This is a myth, by the way—that buying and holding is the way to build your portfolio. But for now let's *just call it really bad advice*, again on average.) Not everyone will tell you to buy and hold, of course, especially investment advisers who make a commission on your trades in stocks. They absolutely love lots of trading. At full commission brokerages, in particular, your broker might make as much on commissions as you'll make on the appreciation of your stock. Lots of people will tell you they've had that experience. But perhaps you're paying them for other things than just picking stocks. I hope so!

If you buy and hold and then in the second year the funds perform exactly opposite of the first year, you end up exactly where you started. You've made nothing in two years.

Strategy #2: None (chasing a "hot" fund is no strategy at all). If your strategy is buying whatever did well last year, that's another non-strategy. You say, "Fund XYZ is the hot fund," close ABC, and shift all your money to the hot fund. Now, in the same scenario, with the funds flip-flopping returns, you'd be down $7,500 after two years.

If you were a gymnast, the crowd would have just groaned and the announcers would be saying something like, "It's so disappointing. She's worked

	Fund ABC	Fund XYZ	Total Value	Return
Investment	$ 10,000	$ 10,000	$ 20,000	
1st Year	x −0.5	x 2		
Value	$ 5,000	$ 20,000	$ 25,000	25%
Hold	$ 5,000	$ 20,000		
2nd Year	x 2	x −0.5		
Value	$ 10,000	$ 10,000	$ 20,000	0%

Strategy #1

	Fund ABC	Fund XYZ	Total Value	Return
Investment	$ 10,000	$ 10,000	$ 20,000	
1st Year	x −0.5	x 2		
Value	$ 5,000	$ 20,000	$ 25,000	25%
Chase	$ 0	$ 25,000		
2nd Year	x 2	x −0.5		
Value	$ 0	$ 12,500	$ 12,500	−37.5%

Strategy #2

so hard for this, but that slip has ended her pursuit of the gold."

This scenario demonstrates the worst of "emotional" investing. Emotional investing is when you get carried away, too excited about the money you're making or missing, and dump your strategy—although most emotional investors (and I'd say the "average" investor fits the description) don't have the patience or the discipline to create a strategy to begin with.

Strategy #3: Rebalance. Now it's time to consider a real strategy. Why did you buy these funds? If you've done your homework and planned properly, you selected them because they provide you with the asset allocation you want. Let's just say that Fund ABC is a large-cap value fund and Fund XYZ is a small-cap growth fund. If you had a strategy that guided your allocation of investments in these two funds and your strategy hasn't changed, wouldn't it still make sense after a year to follow that strategy?

If your strategy still calls for the same investment in these funds, after the first year you'd rebalance them, to make them of equal value again. So you'd move $7,500 from Fund XYZ to Fund ABC. Look what happens now in our scenario. Fund ABC doubles (100% appreciation) and Fund XYZ loses half its value. Because you rebalanced, you now have $31,250—nearly $20,000 more than if you'd invested following your emotions instead of your strategy.

The benefit of rebalancing is that you maintain the asset allocation strategy you created—you stay on the balance beam. The additional benefit is that, over time, with a sound allocation strategy you have the potential to buy low and sell high. Remember: your objective is to create wealth, not just chase the highest possible return on your investment at any one point in time.

How often you should rebalance your portfolio depends in part on whether the investment is taxable or not, the amount invested, time horizon

	Fund ABC	Fund XYZ	Total Value	Return
Investment	$ 10,000	$ 10,000	$ 20,000	
1st Year	x −0.5	x 2		
Value	$ 5,000	$ 20,000	$ 25,000	25%
Rebalance	$ +7,500	$ −7,500		
Value	$ 12,500	$ 12,500		
2nd Year	x 2	x −0.5		
Value	$ 25,000	$ 6,250	$ 31,250	56.25%

Strategy #3

and objective of the investment. I usually rebalance my clients' portfolios, and my own, every six months.

■ IF YOU DRIFT, YOU MAY GO NOWHERE FAST

Now you understand the concept of maintaining your asset allocation with rebalancing. But another danger also arises unless you continuously manage your investments.

Let's go back to Fund XYZ. You selected the fund because it gave you the right asset allocation. In other words, you invested in that fund because it had a certain investment target or style that put it squarely in an asset class that you want in your portfolio. The fund manager would buy only certain types of assets for the fund.

The problem with most retail mutual funds is that the fund managers give themselves a lot of wiggle room. Competition for investors is so intense with some 8,000 funds on the market that fund managers know they have to maintain a certain performance or investors will withdraw their money and invest it in another fund. And it's no wonder that inexperienced investors move their money from fund to fund: in a typical year, 75% of equity mutual funds underperform the S&P 500 index. In the five years from 1995-1999, only 6.83% of open-end, equity mutual funds performed better than the S&P 500! That means that most fund managers consistently perform worse than the market on average.[2]

Because there's no shortage of options for investors looking for better performance, fund managers are tempted to fudge their investment discipline a bit in pursuit of stocks that are hot, even if they are slightly outside the stated investment "style" of the fund, such as growth or value. This is called "style drift" and it's very common. This is one reason that professional money managers or investment advisers with access to institutional funds—funds managed for insurance companies, banks, and other large investors—can offer real value to many individual investors. Institutional funds are often more closely monitored by their institutional investors, so style drift is less pronounced.

Every buy and sell must be monitored carefully to ensure that the fund is adhering to the stated style and not drifting. Continuous management guards against style drift; if drifting occurs, alternative methods are chosen to maintain the desired asset allocation.

■ CONCLUSION

You will certainly be tempted, as we all are, to try to pick the hot stock of next year—which is rarely the hot stock of last year. Avoid that temptation—at least until you have developed a sound strategy for your financial future. Of course there is room in most portfolios for individual stocks. Just remember that, as modern portfolio theory proves, stock picking isn't as important as asset allocation.

---

[2] Mutual fund performance data provided by Lipper, Inc.

The payoff for picking the right stock can be tremendous, but out of a universe of several thousand stocks, picking a really big winner becomes something like a lottery. But if you take a chance in the lottery and you lose, you're out a buck for the ticket. In the stock market, however, if you pick a loser instead of a winner you stand to lose considerably more.

For some people, picking stocks is a little like gambling: it can become almost addictive. If you must indulge your stock-picking fantasies, reserve a little money—a small percentage of your portfolio—and use it to buy a few shares of this or that on speculation. That's what I do; I call it my "moon shot" money.

The real danger of stock picking is that it turns most people into emotional investors. It encourages us to look first at *products* instead of *strategies*—and for most people that places their financial futures in jeopardy. I know it seems to be conservative advice, especially given the unprecedented performance of the stock market in the 1990s, but Newtonian physics rule the investment universe too: the law of gravity still applies—what goes up must come down. The hot stock or even the hot asset class this year will almost certainly not be what's hot next year.

■ HELMER'S HINTS

- Create a strategy first—one based on your wants, not just your needs.
- Answer three important questions:
  1. What type of money am I investing?
  2. What are the tax implications of my investments?
  3. How will I manage my investments?
- Remember the three keys to managing your investments:
  1. Allocate your assets.
  2. Manage your portfolio continuously.
  3. Rebalance your portfolio.
- Never forget the "investing corollary of the real estate rule." The three most important things in investing are allocation, allocation, allocation.

THE MAGIC OF COMPOUNDING INTEREST? THE GAME IS FIXED AND YOU WILL LOSE

The Myth: Your money is safe in fixed interest accounts.

The Reality: Your financial future should lie in diversifying your investments and "accelerating" your money. At least some of it!

I still meet too many people who are living in a distant past when it comes to saving and investing. They still believe in the "magic" of compounding interest—and they dutifully add to their savings accounts each week or month.

You probably have some money somewhere compounding, growing, or accruing in taxable investments. Accumulation of money like this is one of the most widely accepted and embraced concepts in all of personal finance. I learned this at age 12 when I deposited my check from my summer job detassling corn (a tremendous character builder) in my local bank.

The reality is that compounding your earnings is one of the worst things you can do as an investor. As you compound earnings, you compound tax liability. It is grossly inefficient. How then did it come to be so pervasive and endorsed by nearly everyone?

To answer that question, ask yourself who benefits when you leave your money in that investment for a long time? Banks, mutual funds, broker dealers, and insurance companies all want to keep your money as long as they can. Compounding is magic to them. Is it to you?

■ GOOD INTENTIONS, BAD STEWARDSHIP

I'm sure that many fixed-interest investors—although what they're doing is really more saving than investing—note with satisfaction on their monthly or quarterly bank statements the interest earned on their deposits. Their money is making money even as they sleep. It's a comforting thought. But wouldn't it be even more comforting if they were actually making money instead of just keeping ahead of inflation? After paying taxes on those earnings, that compounding interest may not keep pace with the steadily increasing cost of living.

People who put their life savings *only* into fixed-interest investments—all investments that pay a predetermined rate of interest—are as guilty of mismanaging their money as those who race to their computer or the telephone to buy the newest hot stock without any idea of how it fits into their plan or their portfolio.

I know that many people who have only fixed-interest investments do it with good intentions. Their actions are based in what they consider to be the virtues of prudence and frugality. Our culture has no shortage of cautionary tales that teach the virtues of slow and steady progress. The best known is the story of the tortoise and the hare. Slow and steady, the tortoise wins the race after all.

The conservatism that keeps many people in fixed-interest investments is often associated with conservative spending habits. I applaud those people for not spending wildly, but I wish they would be a little more aggressive—dare I say, a little more responsible—with their investing. Even the Bible, in the parable of the 10 talents, suggests that earning a good return on one's assets is good stewardship. In my opinion, there is no virtue in accepting lower returns on your savings than you have to. Put differently, you could be investing, not just saving.

■ DON'T BET THE FARM ON THE NEXT HOT .COM STOCK

If you have most or all of your savings in fixed-interest investments, I'm not encouraging you to take risks you're not comfortable taking. And I don't believe I'm simply caught up in the mania for investing in stocks that has gripped the world in the 1990s. Stock markets have had an unprecedented run for nearly a decade and history teaches us that at some point that run will end. Stock prices will drop and people who have not created their portfolios wisely will lose a great deal of

Average Returns 1926 to 1999*

Investment Type	Average Annual Return
Small Company Stocks	12.6%
Large Company Stocks (S&P 500)	11.3%
Long-Term Government Bonds	5.1%
Treasury Bills	3.7%
Inflation (CPI)	3.1%

Calculations include reinvestment of earnings. Past performance does not guarantee future results. Also refer to Chapter 10 for key differences between these types of investments or asset classes.

*Source: *Stocks, Bonds, Bills and Inflation*® *2000 Yearbook*, ©2000 Ibbotson Associates, Inc. Based on copyrighted works by Ibbotson and Sinquefield. All rights reserved. Used with permission.

Figure 3.1

money. But in many cases the money they lose will be money they wouldn't have had without taking some chances on markets. And if they have rebalanced their portfolios, not all of their winnings will still be on the table.

Contrary to the contentions of some very conservative savers, history is on the side of those whose investment universe goes beyond fixed-interest accounts. In any short period of time, historical returns may not be reached, or they may be wildly exceeded—as has been the case in the 1990s.

Of course, anyone can cite horror stories, like the Crash of 1929 that led to despair for investors and began a nearly decade-long depression. But history has a longer sweep. The same people whose saving habits were conditioned by the Great Depression, those who experienced it and those who passed its lessons on to their children, have also lived through the most prosperous era in the history of the world. It's unfair and unwise to view the world through events that are atypical or historical aberrations.

If you have your savings in fixed-interest investments, perhaps you deserve a pat on the back too. You have something in your portfolio that everyone should have. I dislike them only when they become too much of a good thing. But are they needed in a portfolio? Yes.

As we've already discussed, asset allocation is the key to any financial plan. Fixed-interest investments are an important asset class that balances or provides a hedge against more aggressive asset classes. Interest-earning accounts are one of the asset classes that every investor must consider. The problem arises when it is the only asset class that you own or is the majority of your investment portfolio.

■ FIXED-INTEREST INVESTMENTS MAY BE DETRIMENTAL TO YOUR FINANCIAL HEALTH

Many Americans invest a very high percentage of their money in fixed-interest accounts, because they are looking for safety; they don't want to risk losing their hard-earned money. They believe that investments that are fixed will be safe and secure and will not be volatile. Unfortunately, fixed-interest investments can be as volatile as any other—and the costliest in lost opportunities.

The interest rates offered by fixed-interest investments are relatively similar and very low as of this writing. Additionally, the rate changes constantly, rising and falling with inflation. You may recall that in the early 1980s rates on certificates of deposit (CDs) ran as high as 12% to 15%. Those rates were not as attractive as they seemed, however, because they were negated by runaway inflation of 15% or higher.

In 1981, the average rate earned on a CD was 15.5%. Therefore, $10,000 invested would have earned $1,550 in a year. However, by 1986 the average CD rate was only 7%. If someone rolled over or renewed that CD then, the same $10,000 invested would have generated only $700 per year in earnings. This is significant because the typical CD buyers are conservative and either nearing retirement or already retired. They often depend on the earnings from their investments to subsidize their retirement income. Therefore, in 1986, many had to either reduce their standard of living from the previous five years or, worse, use some of their principal and run the risk of outliving their money. Why did the rate on CDs drop? Because inflation slowed. Does that mean that prices returned to 1981 levels? Of course not. It just means that the rate at which prices were increasing had slowed.

Many retirees are going broke and they don't know why. They invested safely and thought they were doing everything right. Unfortunately, they didn't understand that CDs can be very volatile investments because when the term of the CD expires the fixed rates available for rollover or replacement can be, and often are, lower than the previous rate. Thus, over the long term, CD income streams are unpredictable and, ironically, as uncertain as returns from the stock market. (Remember: unlike stocks, CDs are FDIC-insured.)

With a portfolio of only fixed-interest investments, you will never run the risk of losing any of your principal, as could happen with more aggressive investments. But you run a potentially greater risk of having to use your principal. If you plan to live off the earnings from your investments and the return

is not high enough to support your cost of living, you have no choice but to cut back or spend the principal. To me that risk is much, much scarier than the calculated risk of investing in a mix of volatile assets that, while also conservative, provides a reasonable possibility for greater return.

■ A GOOD ALTERNATIVE TO BONDS

While writing about fixed-interest investments, I would be remiss if I did not mention that in many cases bonds are inappropriate. For investors who like bonds as a source of income or as a hedge against equities as one component of their asset allocation, I strongly encourage considering real estate in the form of a real estate investment trust (REIT). REITs have many advantages over bonds, including:

- Tax advantages. While the before-tax yields on bonds and real estate investment trusts may be comparable, REITs allow for depreciation on the underlying real estate. Thus the after-tax returns can be higher on REITs.

- Lower volatility. Bonds are less volatile than equities; however, the old expression "you can't get blood out of a turnip" is very true. If a corporation cannot pay its bills, what recourse does the bondholder have? Oh yeah, that turnip thing. However, in most REITs the leasing corporation is a secured creditor, so if a corporation defaults on a lease payment or vacates the property, the REIT still has a tangible asset, the underlying property. The REIT can either lease the property to another party or sell the property if the price is right.

- Income increases. Escalation clauses in leases should provide an income for the investor that increases steadily in any market cycle.

- Upside potential. Bonds have a predetermined fixed return. That return can only go down but not up. Real estate, on the other hand, has not only the increase from lease escalation, but also the appreciation potential of the underlying property values. This "equity kicker" has the potential to drive the overall return of the REIT to be competitive with equities without some of the risk exposure of equities.

I recommend, if you want to allocate resources to fixed-interest investments to offset the risks of stocks, that you look into REITs. They are offered publicly and privately. In either case, I advise a REIT that is not so dependent on underlying property values. Real estate prices can fluctuate like the stock market. Real estate prices can fluctuate significantly with downturns in regional economies as well as the national economy. If the performance of your REIT is volatile, like the stock market can be, that undermines the purpose of the REIT. The goal is a steady, competitive, and increasing rate of return.

■ IS RETIREMENT THE TIME TO GET CONSERVATIVE? (MYTH ALERT!!!)

If you're within five years of retiring, it's time to take your money out of stocks or more aggressive mutual funds and move it into something safer, like CDs or a savings account. Have you heard that one? It's *another myth* that has cost many retirees over the years. How close you are to retiring isn't relevant when considering changes to your investments. Of far greater consequence is whether you will need to tap the earnings from your investments to cover your living costs—and how long before you have to do that.

Some people have alternate sources of retirement income, such as a pension and Social Security, that will pay their basic living costs well into their retirement. If you don't believe you will have to tap into your investments for several years, you may not need to alter your asset allocation significantly. And even if you do alter that allocation, the right mix of asset classes will still provide a solid return, and reduce the risk of losing your nest egg, without resorting to converting all of your investments into fixed-interest investments.

Those who retired in the early 1990s, heeded the myth, and took all their investments out of the stock markets would have missed an opportunity to grow their retirement savings significantly—and give themselves a much larger cushion for their later years.

Before we move on to discuss the best

way to use money—to keep it moving —let's consider for just a moment one of the biggest variables in any financial plan: inflation.

■ IS INFLATION ONE OF YOUR BIGGEST WORRIES? (MYTH ALERT!!!)

If inflation is among your top worries, you've succumbed to another of the great myths that can cause harm to your financial future. This is perhaps the *most widely believed myth of all.*

Inflation is the word used to describe the increase in cost of living. It is one of the most overused and overrated aspects of traditional financial planning. Inflation exists—there is no doubt of that. However, it is extremely difficult, virtually impossible, to quantify the inflation rate for any one person or family.

The inflation rate that we see cited most often is the Consumer Price Index (CPI). The historical increase in the CPI has averaged 3.1% per year from 1926 to 1999. Unfortunately, CPI is simply based on the prices of a "basket" of goods and services, a sampling of the things many people buy, so it may not be relevant to your personal cost of living.

All we have to do is examine the changes in college and health care costs—both much higher than 3.1%— to realize that the CPI is really a political tool and not valid in many people's lives. Saying that the inflation rate is 3.1% is a little like saying that the aver-

age family has 2.5 children. The statistical average applies to no one.

Furthermore, to use inflation to determine how much money we will want in the future is a huge error, since no one ever knows with certainty his or her future cost of living. The most important point to understand about inflation is simply that a dollar in the future will not buy as much as it buys today.

Finally, inflation is beyond our individual control. We cannot do anything about price increases. The way to combat inflation is to control your personal spending and use efficient investment strategies designed to outperform the inflation rate.

■ THE REAL GOAL: THE ACCELERATION OF MONEY

Stagnant water becomes dirty and polluted. It loses its value because we cannot consume it or wash with it. However, a flowing stream is an invaluable and endless resource. The same can be said of money. Stagnant, motionless money, even though it may be earning a high rate of return, has potentially less value than money kept in motion. By accelerating your money, you make it work harder for you and accomplish more. Not only do you grow your assets, you also protect them without incurring any additional cost.

Banks understand the acceleration of money. It's how they perform magic with your fixed-interest deposits! Let's assume you walk into a bank and put

$10,000 on deposit in a three-year CD. Your neighbor comes in after you and receives a $10,000 loan. He essentially receives the same $10,000 that you deposited. Your neighbor then buys $10,000 worth of inventory for his business. Finally, the woman he buys his inventory from deposits the $10,000 back into the same bank. We have now completed a full circle, which increases the bank's profits. In fact, the bank attempts to circulate every dollar it receives back into the economy as often as possible, each time enhancing its profit. This acceleration of money concept completely contradicts what the banks tell their customers to do with their money. They advise them to leave their money in the bank to take advantage of the "magic" of compounding interest.

Now let's flip the calendar ahead two years. You need $10,000 to expand your business. You go back to the same bank and discover a substantial penalty for early withdrawal on your CD. The bank suggests you use the CD as collateral for a loan. You agree to a $10,000 loan at 12% interest while your CD is simultaneously earning a hypothetical 6%. As ludicrous as it sounds, people do things like this every day because they allow their money to become stagnant.

I want to explore a specific example to demonstrate the inefficiency of accumulating or compounding money, while illustrating the efficiency of the acceleration of money strategy. First, however, I must introduce an important economic concept that's critical to efficient financial planning and understanding the acceleration of money.

■ EVEN GOOD INVESTMENTS MAY COST YOU

One of the most frequently overlooked economic concepts in traditional personal finance is opportunity cost. Any time you have a cost in your financial world, you have not only that cost but also the added cost of missing an opportunity to do something else with those dollars. For example, if you owe me $1, but I forgive the debt, you can now put the dollar in your bank and earn 5%. At the end of one year you will have $1.05. However, if you had paid your debt to me, you not only would have been out the dollar, but you also would not have had the ability to earn the five cents.

Another example would be a doctor who earns $1,000 every day he goes to work. If he takes a day off to take his family to an amusement park and that event costs him $200, what is his actual cost? If your answer is $1,200 dollars, you are correct! That's a lot of amusement. The doctor not only has the cost of the event, $200, but also the cost of not working—$1,000.

Opportunity cost exists whenever there are choices. You must consider the potential benefit of the choice you reject. A financial plan that does not consider opportunity cost is not economically sound. Opportunity cost is real dollars.

A savings account provides an excellent example. Let's say you deposit your savings in a bank account that earns a hypothetical 4%, a typical bank rate as of this writing. You are paying a price for maintaining that account—the opportunity cost—or the difference between what you are earning and what you could be earning. Even another conservative investment, such as a short-term U.S. Treasury bond, would pay you 5%, for example. In it's simplest form that means your opportunity cost is 5% (potential)—4% (actual) or 1%.

If we assume you have $10,000 in a 5% savings account, you would earn $500 in interest in a year. If you could have invested that money at 7% in another investment—perhaps without unduly increasing the risk—you could have earned $700 in the same year or a difference of $200. That may not seem like a lot of money, but if you leave that extra $200 in a 7% account, and do the same every year for 15 years, you now have an extra $5,500. And if you had been willing to be a little more aggressive, perhaps you could have earned a 9% return or you could have divided your $10,000 among several investments—asset allocation, remember—and perhaps pushed your overall return even higher, without accepting an unreasonable amount of risk.

Multiply the opportunity cost by the amount you may have in such accounts and the sums become significant to your lifestyle and your dreams. Multiply the opportunity cost by thousands of people who maintain too much of their savings in fixed-interest investments and the numbers become staggering. Bankers and others who reinvest the money you leave stagnant in such accounts would not be pleased if all of you withdrew your money!

Opportunity cost exists whenever going with one alternative precludes another. This "either/or" approach to investing should be a part of your review of every investment vehicle and, as we shall see now, the tax consequences of every investment.

■ THE LEAST APPRECIATED OPPORTUNITY COST: TAXES!

Nobody likes to pay taxes. Regardless of the role you believe government should play in society and our individual lives, it hurts when you have to write your checks to the IRS or see how much of your paycheck is withheld for taxes.

But let's look at taxes from an investment perspective—and as I suggested in Chapter 2, if you don't consider tax consequences, your financial plan is woefully incomplete and inadequate.

When you pay income taxes, your rate of return from the IRS is 0% in actual dollars. If you could eliminate or reduce your taxes, you would have not only the tax savings but also the ability to invest those savings and earn money from them. This would create an opportunity gain. However, most people pay their taxes and complain about overpaying and never realize that the compounded lost opportunity over time can exceed their actual tax payments. We will discuss later on how understanding and acting on this concept can greatly enhance your investment performance in your financial plan.

Imagine that we walk into our local bank and our banker makes us the following unbelievable offer that's too good to be true. For a $50,000 deposit the bank will pay an astronomical 15% interest. Furthermore, this account is totally liquid, it has full FDIC insurance, and there's no market risk. The bank even guarantees us that the interest rate cannot go down, but can only go up. Sign me up! By almost any measuring stick, this would be an outstanding investment. In fact, it's so good it doesn't exist. But bear with me for a minute and let's pretend that it does in order to make a point.

What are the results of this hypothetical investment? (See Figure 3.2.) At 15%, the $50,000 earns $7,500 in the

Accumulation Strategy

Year	Deposit	Value	Earnings*	Taxes
1	$50,000		$7,500	
2		57,500	8,625	$2,625
3		66,125	9,919	3,019
4		76,044	11,407	3,472
5		87,451	13,118	3,992
6		100,568	15,085	4,591
7		115,653	17,348	5,280
8		133,001	19,950	6,072
9		152,951	22,943	6,983
10		175,894	26,384	8,030
11		202,278	30,342	9,234
12		232,620	34,893	10,620
13		267,513	40,127	12,213
14		307,639	46,146	14,044
15		353,785	53,068	16,151
		406,853		18,574
Total			**$356,853**	**$(124,899) = Net earnings $231,954**

* For illustration only; does not represent any specific investment. Remember this is a hypothetical investment that's too good to be true.

Figure 3.2

first year. Assuming a combined federal and state tax of 35%, the tax liability on the $7,500 earnings is $2,625.

To keep the accounting simpler, let's assume the taxes are paid from somewhere else in our financial world, from some other account. We could take earnings off the bank account to pay taxes, but in my experience, people seldom do that. I can count on one hand the number of times someone has said, "I'm liquidating shares of my mutual fund to pay the taxes on my mutual fund." Furthermore, if this hypothetical investment were earning 15% with no market risk, we probably wouldn't want to take money from it.

Fast-forward 15 years into the future. Because of the "magic" of compounding interest, 15 years later the hypothetical account value is $406,853. We've hypothetically earned $356,853. Not bad even in a dream world! But unfortunately we've also paid $124,899 in taxes. After paying taxes, our net gain is $231,954.

Now let's calculate the opportunity cost of paying all that money in taxes. If we could eliminate the taxes on the earnings and instead invest that money at 15% too, which we just agreed was too good to be true, at the end of 15 years we'd have another $278,606! That's the opportunity cost of paying taxes in this case. It seems a steep price to pay for our net earnings of $231,954. When looked at in that light, our hypo-

thetical investment no longer looks quite as impressive. But the problem is not the investment. The problem is the strategy of *accumulation.*

Of course, in the real world, we can't refuse to pay taxes on our gains, so this calculation of opportunity cost is not completely realistic. But there is a way we can reduce our taxes and recapture some of that opportunity cost.

Remember: we said that the problem with compounding interest in a taxable account is that we also accumulate tax liability. So, let's see what happens if we "accelerate" our money. At a glance this won't make sense—but bear with me.

We can deploy an acceleration strategy that will make our money much more efficient. Using this strategy, the annual earnings are distributed or accelerated from the taxable account into a tax-free investment, let's say a municipal bond that pays 5%. Once again, we'll pay the *taxes* out-of-pocket. Distributing the earnings prevents the taxes from compounding, too. The tax is not completely eliminated, but it's greatly reduced because it has been flattened. The tax savings, which start in the second year, can now be invested, too. I know it doesn't sound logical to take money out of a taxable account, even if that account is earning an unbelievable 15% and put it into an account that earns only 5% tax-free. But let's look at the numbers and you'll see that we come out ahead. (Figure 3.3.)

free investment that could have potentially netted us a total of $41,000 more than leaving assets to accumulate in a taxable bank account that earned 15% per year? That wonderful investment is one that the financial "experts" will tell you not to use: *variable universal life insurance.* In all cases, these rates of return are for illustration only and do not represent any specific investment nor do they guarantee that specific returns could be achieved. Keep reading; in Chapter 7 I will tell you why another widely accepted myth might lead you to overlook what may be an excellent opportunity for you.

The conclusion is perfectly clear, painfully clear if you've been accumulating assets in taxable accounts: accumulating or compounding earnings in a taxable account is *not* an efficient strategy. The *big lie* about the magic of compounding in a stagnant, taxable account has been fed to an unknowing consuming public for decades. Of course, the example I've just provided makes some assumptions that simplify accounting—and accounting is rarely simple in the real world. But even if you changed some of the details or assumptions, the larger point remains valid: by looking at opportunity cost, including taxes paid, and accelerating your money instead of letting your tax liability compound, you may be able to improve the efficiency of your investments.

■ CONCLUSION

Compounding interest in taxable fixed-interest accounts can be very costly to you. Such an investment strategy could prevent you from realizing the true potential of your savings and investments and, therefore, your dreams. Your earnings compound, yes, but so does your tax liability, which represents an opportunity cost that too many people overlook.

That great bugaboo—inflation—is not nearly as great a threat to your financial security as stagnant money. Fixed-interest investments are, of course, an important asset class that, in combination with others, can reduce your investment risk and optimize your returns. But fixed-interest investments should be only a small portion of any investment portfolio. They are more volatile than most people acknowledge and the opportunity cost associated with them is intolerable. Moreover, modern portfolio theory has clearly demonstrated that there are far more efficient ways to reduce overall portfolio risk.

If you're committed to fixed-interest investments, consider real estate investment trusts, which offer greater opportunities for appreciation although they do involve a possible loss of principal.

Money sitting in compounding fixed interest accounts is a banker's dream. No wonder they've always called it magic—and convinced an unquestioning public that it is. Do not as they say, but as they do: accelerate your money.

■ HELMER'S HINTS

- Avoid "emotional investing," which can be governed by fear as much as greed.

- Don't limit your portfolio to only fixed-interest investments. They may not be as safe as you think—and the opportunity cost might be killing you.

- Accelerate your money, instead of letting taxable interest compound. Compounding taxable interest is inefficient because the tax liability compounds too.

4

Prepaying Your Mortgage Is Like Throwing Away Money

The Myth: You save a lot of money by prepaying your mortgage.

The Reality: You'd be far better off investing the extra mortgage payments.

A home mortgage is one of the most efficient obligations you can make. The government makes it so. It's the biggest tax deduction most people can get—and by far the biggest of all government subsidies. The tax deduction that you get from your home mortgage interest makes it an extremely efficient way to borrow money—and invest it.

But most debt is horribly harmful to your financial future. Remember our discussion of opportunity cost? Even investments that appear very attractive may have some opportunity cost. Imagine the opportunity cost of consumer debt! You're not only paying interest, but also forfeiting the ability to earn a return on those dollars if you could have invested them instead. The cost of consumer debt becomes staggering—and the only purpose it serves for most people is to enable them to buy things a few months earlier than if they had saved the money to pay in cash.

If you have consumer debt, with interest rates these days in the 12%-21% range, you are essentially paying 12%-21% more for every purchase you make until you pay off that debt. Any dollar you spend instead of applying it toward your balance is a borrowed dollar. If you're buying a loaf of bread that's priced at $1.50, it's actually costing you $1.80 if you have a credit balance at 20% interest on a credit card somewhere. And the craziest thing of all is that some people charge things to credit cards just because those things happen to be on sale at the moment. To save 15%, they're willing to pay 20% in interest. Go figure!

■ DEBTOR'S PRISON

Debt is the first matter any financial plan has to address. Millions of Americans have inefficient debt. Consumer debt and personal bankruptcies are at all-time highs. Millions of Americans carry balances on high-interest, non-deductible credit cards and never seem to gain ground. They can't eliminate that debt—and they have a devil of a time even reducing it.

I've seen firsthand how deep a hole some people can dig for themselves with consumer debt. One of the more extreme examples was a couple I'll call Phil and Lil. They came to me because they wanted to purchase their dream home. The home cost $250,000, which wasn't out of their reach because they had a combined annual income of $150,000. But when they went to get financing for the home they wanted, they were turned down by more than one lender. The reason? More than $100,000 of credit card debt—money for which they were paying 16% on average. Every month the interest cost alone on that debt, without paying a penny toward the principal, was more than $1,300.

Most Americans don't have that much of a problem with plastic money, but it's not unusual to see people with credit card debt at levels that will keep them from *ever* investing a penny unless they radically change their spending habits.

The first step in controlling debt is to control spending. You do not need to buy a new jungle gym for your kids just because your neighbor did. Keeping up with the Joneses is very dangerous and can cause irreparable financial harm. Remember that credit cards are not a replacement for cash. They are for convenience so you need not always carry cash. If you don't have the cash to pay the balance in full when the statement comes, you can't afford the purchase. That's all there is to it. I'm sorry if that means you must wait a few months for that new bedroom furniture or go without a vacation this year, but it's for your own good.

■ A DEBT LIKE NO OTHER

If you've incurred inefficient debt, one method of eliminating it is to transfer the debt to your home equity. The most efficient debt offers a long payback period, low interest rates, and deduction of the interest on your income tax. A mortgage is the only way of achieving all three of those goals.

Many people are reluctant to use their home equity to consolidate other debt. This reluctance really stems from a mind set that's behind the times. Sure, 30 years ago, if people refinanced their home or took out a second mortgage, you can be sure that the neighbors were talking behind their backs about their financial woes. But using your home's equity is economically wise. It provides low interest rates, a tax deduction, and an extended amortization.

However, even this form of debt should not be used recklessly. Defaulting on a mortgage of any kind has greater consequences than defaulting on consumer loans. Mortgage loans are secured by your home, which means that if you can't make payments, you will lose your home. Consumer credit lenders can't take such drastic remedies.

In fact, buying the use of money today through a mortgage is so efficient that I recommend making the smallest possible down payment when you buy a house and carrying the largest mortgage that you can. Consider this: in the latter half of the 1990s, you could get a 30-year fixed mortgage for about 7%-8% interest. Depending on your tax bracket, after taking your interest deduction your net "cost" of that money would have been 4%-6%. Could you have invested the extra money not used for a down payment and averaged better than 6% net after taxes? You certainly could have.

A simpler way to think about this is to disregard taxes. In other words, you finance at 7% and don't consider the deduction. The historical average annual return of the S&P 500 is about 10.4%. Economically it makes sense to try to invest as soon as possible and apply less money to this debt. Using these hypothetical figures, you would have a net pretax gain on these dollars of 3.4%.

The price of borrowing money fluctuates, of course, as does the price of anything else. If mortgage interest rates were to rise above 10% again, as they did in the 1980s, you'd have to compare carefully the potential net gain or loss of any down payment or prepayment plan. But if you were among those who financed or refinanced in the 1990s at around 7%, you will almost certainly do better investing that money instead of paying down your mortgage.

But, you say, what if you figure in the appreciation of the real estate? That has to be worth something, too. It is—but your home will appreciate at the same rate regardless of how much equity you have in it. It does not appreciate faster if you have more equity. In fact, if your home does appreciate, you earn a far higher return on your investment if your down payment is lower.

Suppose you are going to purchase a home for $100,000. You can actually get financing with 5% down, or $5,000, but you're considering putting down $20,000 or 20%. What will happen if your home appreciates by 5% the first year? With $5,000 down, you would have a return on paper of 100%. With a down payment of $20,000, however, your return would be only 25%.

The stock market historically appreciates faster than real estate anyway. If you put less money down and invest the difference in an equity portfolio, you would have the potential to eliminate the mortgage faster!

One catch in making lower down payments is that many lenders require mortgage insurance until the borrower has 20% equity in the property. Look carefully at the cost of that mortgage insurance to compare it with the cost of a lower down payment. Or better yet, find a mortgage lender that doesn't require mortgage insurance. Some home buyers have even found that it's cheaper to take out a second mortgage immediately to cover the difference between the down payment and the 20% equity requirement, just to eliminate the high premiums of mortgage insurance.

■ 15-YEAR VERSUS 30-YEAR MORTGAGE

The same principle applies to the question of whether to take a 15-year or 30-year mortgage. With the low interest rates of recent years, many people have been able to afford the larger monthly payments of a shorter-duration mortgage. Therefore, they have opted for a 15-year mortgage in order to eliminate the debt twice as fast and save thousands in interest costs. That's a bad choice—at least if they have the discipline to take the difference in the monthly payments and invest it.

Even though a loan may be amortized over a 30-year period, nothing prevents us from paying it off early. If we take a 30-year mortgage and invest the difference between its smaller payment and what our payment would have been on a 15-year mortgage schedule, we actually need only a very modest rate of return in order to make a balloon payment on our 30-year mortgage after 15 years. (See Figure 4.1.)

the S&P 500 over the last 50 years is 10.4%. If you earned that return over the 15 years, you would be able to pay off your 30-year mortgage after 15 years and still have several thousand dollars left in your investment account. Moreover, you would have enjoyed the flexibility of smaller payments over that time in the event of an emergency such as disability or loss of employment.

Even if you earned only just enough on your investment to make the balloon payment—meaning that you had

The Advantages of a Longer Mortgage

You might end up money ahead if you take out a 30-year mortgage instead of a 15-year mortgage—if you invest the difference in payments. This example is for a $100,000 mortgage at 7.125% for the 30-year obligation and 6.875% for the 15-year mortgage.

	30-Year Mortgage	15-Year Mortgage
Loan Balance	$100,000	$100,000
Interest Rate	7.125%	6.875%
Annual Payment	$ 8,089	$10,702
Principal Owed		
After 15 Years	$ 74,390	$ 0

Figure 4.1

If you invested the difference between the annual payments, you would need to earn only 5.5% net (after tax) return to accumulate $74,390 after 15 years. That's the equivalent of roughly an 8.5% return before taxes if you were in a combined federal and state tax bracket of 35%. And keep in mind that the average annual return on

to liquidate your investment account to pay off the mortgage early—you would still have enjoyed the greater tax deduction provided over that time by the longer mortgage. Your mortgage interest would have provided tax deductions of $33,502 instead of $21,187 with the shorter mortgage.

Of course, all of these benefits disappear if you don't have the discipline to invest the difference in payments. In addition, you need to consider the risk involved in investing; the returns will fluctuate and there is the possibility of loss of principal. If you need the threat of foreclosure to force you to set aside the money each month, you're better off to take the shorter mortgage, if you can afford it. And set this book down now, because without that discipline you're never going to get far enough ahead to think about saving and investing anyway!

A very popular scam that the mortgage companies are running now is to have the borrower make biweekly payments rather than monthly or 13 payments per year instead of 12. They then demonstrate how you will pay off your mortgage in 23 years instead of 30 and save thousands of dollars in interest. Of course, they often charge a fee to provide this service. What a joke!

This makes no sense, for at least two reasons. First, some companies are charging as much as $400 to set up this change in payments. Even if it did make sense to accelerate your mortgage, you can pay extra on your principal anytime you'd like; you shouldn't have to pay a fee to increase your mortgage payment. Second, as we have already demonstrated, those same dollars invested have the potential to earn a higher return than the interest rate at which you're borrowing for your mortgage. Thus, paying off the debt early may be achieved more efficiently by investing and using your investment to retire the debt, rather than putting extra dollars toward the debt service.

■ A FINANCIAL CROWBAR

You know how a crowbar works. It's a lever that enables you to move things or pull out nails that you couldn't budge with your own strength. Leverage is the term that means the same thing in financial circles: it's the crowbar that moves money.

The best illustration is perhaps the example above about making a down payment of $5,000 or $20,000 on a home that costs $100,000. If the appreciation on that home is 5% in a year, that's a gain of $5,000 regardless of how much money you put down. Your down payment was your crowbar, your leverage. It's what gave you ownership of a $100,000 asset and any appreciation on that asset.

It's a concept that is often used in finance and investing. Many investors play with the concept through stock and commodities options or margin purchases of stocks. In those cases, an investor puts up a portion of the money to buy assets or the future option to buy assets at a set price, like a down payment, and assumes a debt for the remaining cost of those assets. If the assets appreciate significantly, the investor can sell the assets at the higher price, pay off the money borrowed to buy those assets, and pocket the difference. If the assets depreciate, however, the investor could be forced to put up the entire amount to buy those assets at their original higher price. It's a high-risk use of debt that doesn't have a place in the portfolios of most investors. Investors can make a fortune in a short time, but they can also be wiped out financially if one transaction goes bad.

■ CONCLUSION

Debt is often the destroyer of dreams. But mortgage debt can help you realize your dreams, not only because of where you live, but also because of how you can save and invest. Mortgage loans are different from all other types of loans, because the interest is typically lower than for other forms of debt and the interest is tax-deductible. That combination makes mortgage debt very attractive. Rather than pay off your mortgage as soon as you can, invest the difference and you will have the potential to come out ahead. The amount you will earn on your investment could exceed the amount you pay in additional interest.

Avoid all other kinds of debt, including the high-risk debt of stock margin purchases and stock and commodities options. Leave those investments to the professional gamblers. Otherwise, buy only what you can pay for with cash.

■ HELMER'S HINTS

• Eliminate all debt—except your home mortgage. The first step in any financial plan should be to pay off any outstanding consumer debt. Unless your investments are earning a higher rate of return—after taxes—than you are paying in consumer debt interest, your investments are still losing money.

• You may be able to pay off your mortgage faster, if you make minimum regular mortgage payments and invest the money that you could apply to prepaying your mortgage. Based on historical averages (no guarantee of future performance!), your rate of return on that investment has the potential to be higher than the interest rate on your mortgage.

• Consolidate consumer debt in a home equity mortgage. Home equity loans charge lower interest than consumer loans and the interest is tax-deductible in most cases.

5

If You're a Disciplined Saver, You're Above Averaging

The Myth: Investing a little each month is the best way to ensure that you buy stocks or mutual funds at the best price.

The Reality: Dribbling your money into the market is inefficient—and you're as likely to miss rallies as you are to miss dips in prices.

If your biggest concern is *when* to invest your money, you're worrying about the wrong thing. Investing a set amount each month is fine as a *saving* strategy, but as an *investing* strategy, it's faulty.

In the first four chapters, we looked at 1) getting what you want, not what you need; 2) the need for a financial plan—a strategy; 3) the inefficiency of investing in only fixed interest investments, and 4) the right and wrong ways to use debt. So maybe I've convinced you that you need to be invested in equity and fixed-interest markets—once you have your non-mortgage debt cleared up. Good. Now we have to decide the timing for those investments. Right?

Well there's not much to decide. The best time to invest is as soon as you can.

If you've created your asset allocation strategy, invest now!

But many people don't follow that advice, or they try to beat the market by picking the right *time* to invest. The two most popular methods of trying to beat the market that way are dollar-cost averaging and market timing.

■ DOLLAR COST AVERAGING IS OVERRATED!

Dollar cost averaging is a nugget of misguided "wisdom" that seems to be promoted primarily by mutual fund companies—although it has it's advocates among TV financial news readers whose qualification for giving investment advice seems to be good hair.

Here's how dollar-cost averaging works: rather than investing money in stocks or mutual funds in one lump sum, you invest a set amount of money every month. The thinking is that since the dollar amount remains consistent, the investor acquires more shares when prices are low and fewer when share prices are high. The supposed advantage is that the average price the consumer pays is less than the average price at which the security is offered.[3]

---

[3] Here's what the regulators have to say: "Periodic investment plans do not assure a profit or protect loss in a declining market. Dollar-cost averaging involves continuous investment in securities regardless of the fluctuating price of such securities. Investors should carefully consider their ability to continue their investments during periods of low price levels." Don't you love the way lawyers write?

It works like this. In successive months we invest $100 into a mutual fund. The first month the share price is $10. Therefore, we buy 10 shares. The second month, the share price is only $5. Consequently, we buy 20 shares. To calculate the average share price of the fund at the time we made our purchases we add the prices the fund was offered at and divide by the number of purchases ($10 + $5 ÷ 2 = $7.5). The average share price is $7.50. However, we spent $200 to acquire 30 shares, meaning our average purchase price per share was only $6.67 (200 ÷ 30).

That seems like a pretty good deal—if that's all the further you care to go in analyzing your costs. But the fact remains that your 30 shares are not worth $6.67 a share, they are now worth only $5 a share. If the share price then bounces back up, your purchase at $5 a share will look good. But what if it goes down further? Then wouldn't you have been better off to have just kept your money in the bank until you knew share prices would go up? But if you did know the price would go up from $5, why did you buy only 20 shares at that price?

Conversely, what if the original share price had increased by 50% from one month to the next, instead of decreasing by that amount—and continued to go up every month after that? Then dollar-cost averaging wouldn't look so good, either. If you'd had the money to invest, you would have been far better off investing it all at the beginning.

The people who recommend dollar-cost averaging say, "You don't know what the market will do, and you're crazy to guess, so hedge your bets by investing a little at a time. You won't miss out on long rallies or get hurt as badly by a big crash."

It's true that markets are as likely to go up as down on any given day, but we do know that over time markets have consistently gone up. Although, again, past performance does not guarantee future results, the historical average annual increase for the S&P 500 is 10.4%. It seems that if you really want to play the law of averages you'd want your money in the market sooner rather than later.

While the popular perception of markets is that they increase steadily and plummet suddenly, research provides an interesting counterpoint. The most precipitous collapses of markets have occurred on single infamous days such as Black Monday in 1929 and Black Tuesday in 1987. But research demonstrates that one-day rallies can have an enormous impact on overall performance as well.

If you take just the best 30 days away from the 2,500-plus trading days in the ten-year period from 1987-1996, the average annual return drops by two-thirds—from 15.3% to just 5.2% per year. (Figure 5.1.) That's if you missed, on average, only 3 trading days a year for that ten-year period! Dollar-cost averagers are going to miss some of these big days too, just as they avoid some of the big down days. Dollar-cost averaging is guessing with a hedge—with no real rationale at all for the guessing. Perhaps a consistent investment plan such as dollar-cost averaging gives some people the illusion of an investment strategy where none really exists.

So why do people recommend dollar-cost averaging as an investment strategy? Mutual fund companies stand bet that people who dollar-cost average are less likely to withdraw their money from funds when stocks plunge or a fund performs poorly.

Redemptions from mutual funds can get very expensive for those funds if enough shareholders redeem their shares at the same time. If mutual

Don't Miss the Good Days*

	S&P 500 Annualized Returns
1987-1996 (2,593 trading days)	15.3%
Minus the 10 best days	10.5%
Minus the 20 best days	7.7%
Minus the 30 best days	5.2%

*Source: Wellington Management Group, LLP.
The S&P 500 is an unmanaged index; investors cannot invest directly in an index. Remember: Past performance does not guarantee future results.

Figure 5.1

to gain the most if you follow the strategy. Of course, it would be in their interest too if you invest as much as you can with them as soon as you can. But a fund company also wants you to become a regular investor. They want you to get in the habit of adding to your account every month—and they don't want you to be scared off by a little downturn in the market.

Dollar-cost averaging is a wonderful way to keep people invested even if markets are down for a time. It's a theory that encourages people to look at the bright side of bad markets: "Wow, look how cheaply I'm buying shares this month." I couldn't prove it, but I'd

funds don't have enough cash reserves to pay off redemptions, they have to sell assets—and being forced to sell assets when prices are low isn't very good for overall performance. Mutual funds are more profitable for their managers if people invest steadily and consistently over a long period of time, instead of jumping into and out of the funds, even with larger sums.

Dollar-cost averaging is a defensive strategy—a saving strategy—not an efficiency strategy. It is for accumulating assets not *allocating* assets already *accumulated*. It has the potential to work fine for saving $50, $100, and $200 a month—and if you don't have any investments or savings, I'd recommend that you start doing that. But if you already have $5,000, $10,000, or even $20,000 available it is more efficient to invest that money in one lump sum as soon as possible.

■ SECOND-GUESSING, OUT-THINKING, AND UNDERPERFORMING

The more aggressive method of trying to outguess the market doesn't even present the illusion of strategy—it's pure gambling. It's called market timing, which means putting money into or pulling it out of stocks based on whether one thinks the market is going up or down in the short term or even on a given day—or hour!

Investing should not be a guessing game—not at least for those who want to consistently make money. As I described in Chapter 2, Modern Portfolio Theory is based on research that demonstrates that market timing and stock selection *combined* account for less than 10% of a portfolio's success, the rest is due to asset allocation.

Those who reduce investing to guessing market moves are making investing far more complicated and potentially far less rewarding than it should be. You probably know people, as I do, who have picked the right time to make an investment. "I bought the sucker and it went up 30% the next week," they gloat. They probably mention it at all because it was such a rarity in their investment experience. But, like me, I bet you know

very few people, if any, who have *consistently* picked the right time to make an investment. It's tough to replicate good luck. It's tough to know when those 3 big days each year are going to fall.

If market timing were really so simple that your Uncle Wilbur could master it, don't you think that some Wall Street company with millions to spend on computers and software and mathematicians would eventually figure it out too? Well, they haven't—and many high-flying companies and stock pickers have had their comeuppance in bankruptcy court when their theories crashed along with their portfolios.

Too many people try too hard to figure out when to get into and out of markets. Morningstar, Inc., a company that tracks performance of mutual funds, monitored the performance of 219 growth funds for five years ending in 1994 and then researched how well the investors in those funds had done. Over those five years the average aggregate performance of the funds was 12.5% appreciation per year. That's a five-year performance most people would be happy with. Were the investors in the funds during that time happy with the performance? Not likely! Why? The actual return for investors in those funds for that period of time averaged *minus* 2.2%.[4]

The average investor in the funds lost money in the same time period that the funds were appreciating in value. How could that be? Because more investors jumped on board when the funds were

---

[4] Securities Data Publishing, June 1, 1998.

doing well and then got off when they were doing badly. Hot funds had attracted investors, but when they cooled off, investors abandoned them for other hot funds. The investors in those funds, on average, were buying high and selling low—exactly the opposite of every investor's intention.

I had a frustrating experience in the fall of 1998 with an investor trying to time the market. One component of the plan I prepared for this woman was an improved allocation of her assets. Before implementing the plan, however, and buying the assets I recommended, she wanted to discuss it with her brother. That was perfectly understandable, so I agreed to call her in a couple of days to answer any questions that might come up in their discussion of the proposed plan.

I discovered that she was reticent to implement the plan at that time. You see, since mid-July of that year the market had been in a tailspin. The S&P 500 had depreciated about 20%. She was troubled by the markets at that time and wanted to wait until the markets "stabilized" before investing. By November, the market had regained virtually everything it had lost from July to October—and she was still standing on the sidelines waiting for some magical point at which she would know that the markets had stabilized.

She had passed on the opportunity to buy stocks at about a 15% discount from where the price had been earlier in the year and to where it had returned while she was still waiting.

If you were considering buying something for $100 and you were confident it was a good purchase, and then you saw that it was on sale for $85, would you refuse to buy it just because the price had dropped? Of course not. You wouldn't be able to get out your checkbook fast enough. Conversely, if instead of going on sale, the item's price were raised to $115 would you think, "It's even more valuable now, so it's an even better buy?" Unfortunately, when it comes to investments, most people respond like that. They react emotionally, not logically.

One of the greatest benefits of a good financial plan is that it gives you something concrete to cling to when your emotions are about to carry you away.

■ A KISS IS STILL A KISS

A timeless movie, *Casablanca*, gave us a timeless song that contains a line all investor's should keep in mind. Play it, Sam. "A kiss is still a kiss, a sigh is just a sigh, *fundamental things apply as time goes by.*"

I don't see any changes in the fundamentals of investing and markets that came out of the supercharged markets of the 1990s, even though the decade did give us an unprecedented bull market. Could that decade be followed by an unprecedented bear run during which stocks consistently decline in value? Anything is possible in stock markets. Some people think that the fundamentals have changed, which means the bad as well as the good could become more extreme. They could be right, but I doubt it. I think the fundamental things apply.

The S&P 500 has never lost money over any 10-year period since World War II. (And $10,000 invested in the S&P 500 in 1978 would have been worth $262,000 plus in 1998!)[5] Although there is no guarantee, I would expect that the average annual return on money invested in equities will remain not too far from the historical average of just over 10%. That means at some point we will certainly have a couple years of lower returns and slower growth. The investors who will be hurt the worst, will be those who have no strategy, but just chase hot stocks. Investors who have proper asset allocation in their portfolios will have the potential to see a return on their investments that could exceed what they would be getting if they were totally invested in fixed-rate investments. Your asset allocation may give a prominent place to equity investments, but it will also balance those investments with others that are expected to have a negative correlation.

While I don't believe the rules of markets have changed, I think the psychology of investing has changed for the short term. The resilience of markets in the last few years has led some people to believe that investing is easy. But if it were so easy, why is it that 3 out of 4 mutual funds *underperform* the S&P 500 index in a typical year?

I think one could make the case that markets have had a sustained run up precisely because they efficiently channel our society's resources to where they will earn the greatest return. That's a condensed version of Efficient Markets Theory, which is widely embraced among market theorists and academics. But if markets are efficient, and always have been, how do we explain an anomaly or divergence from historical norms such as the bull market of the 1990s?

We could point to many factors—after all, efficiency isn't necessarily simple—but one major factor has been the rapid emergence of an entirely new technology and industry that has changed and will continue to change how we live and how we work. In the early 1980s personal computers were almost unheard of. That's less than 20 years ago. Since then computers have transformed the world. They have increased productivity in so many fields that corporate profits have grown at an impressive pace. At least investors have been impressed.

But also I think consumers have been impressed. The quality of so many things we buy has improved dramatically without an accompanying increase in price. I think that's one of the reasons Wal-Mart and Target have been phenomenally successful retailers. The quality of lower-priced merchandise has improved so drastically that there

---

[5] Source: *Stocks, Bonds, Bills and Inflation*® *2000 Yearbook*, ©2000 Ibbotson Associates, Inc. Based on copyrighted works by Ibbotson and Sinquefield. All rights reserved. Used with permission.

seems to be much less differentiation between low-end and high-end merchandise in many categories. Perhaps the narrowing of the quality gap also accounts for the success of a Nordstrom's, a higher-end retailer that differentiated itself with service and dedication to customer satisfaction. With other competitive advantages shrinking, Nordstrom's stood out by competing on a level that others in their market segment did not or could not.

The new tools and technologies for productivity improvement began to emerge in the 1980s at the same time that American companies faced the most serious competitive challenge ever from foreign companies. It truly was a crisis—and it led to serious upheaval and consequently dramatic improvements in how companies are structured and run. Any stock price, of course, is based primarily on investors' analysis of a company's ability to earn profits in the future. With new productivity tools and improved management, which reduced costs, the prospects for future profits from most companies were brighter.

The advent of personal computers also created the conditions for the emergence of the Internet—a whole new avenue of commerce and entertainment. The race to adapt and create new technologies to harness the enormous potential of computers and the Internet has generated an industrial excitement and energy that may be as unprecedented as the 1990s bull market.

Combine the excitement generated by a booming new industry and the prospect for lucrative returns on investment with productivity increases and events that have kept interest rates low and investment rates high, and you have the conditions for a long bull market.

Does that mean markets have changed forever? Are they so different from 8 years ago that they will never return to old behaviors? I don't think so. What has changed for the time being is the business environment. As computer technologies mature and this burst of industrial creativity wanes, however, that environment will return to a more normal historical situation. Excitement about equity markets will diminish as industries consolidate the advances of the past two decades. Some fortunes will be lost in the process, but for most investors it may well be a calmer, less stressful time. They'll no longer feel compelled to search for stocks that return 100% a year.

For those of us who have had good asset allocation—and regularly rebalanced the excellent returns of recent years—the long bull market has been a windfall. We have been successful not necessarily because we timed the market well or picked hot stocks. We were invested as fully as we could afford to be for as much of that bull market as possible. We were content to take the attractive earnings that history suggested were possible and were very pleasantly surprised by the upside.

Will we give back some of the gains we saw in recent years? Probably we will—at least a little. I don't know about you, but instead of trying to time my exit from the markets if they do begin to slide, I've rebalanced my portfolio to try to take advantage of the negative correlation when it happens. Why be scared when you can be smart?

■ THE STORY OF JACK AND JILL

You probably remember the story of Jack and Jill. When last we visited them they had gone up the hill to fetch some water and Jack accidentally broke his crown. You are probably not aware of much about their lives after that incident.

Jill entered the workforce at age 21 and immediately started to contribute $2,000 per year to an IRA. At age 30 she got married, quit working and no longer contributed to her retirement account. Thus, she contributed $2,000 per year for nine years for a total of $18,000. Her account yielded a hypothetical 10% every year. At age 65 Jill's IRA account was worth $839,556.

Her brother Jack was delayed in getting a good job—largely due to complications from his broken crown. Jack started to contribute to his IRA at age 30. He was able to invest $2,000 per year for 35 years for a total of $70,000 until he retired at age 65. Like Jill, he earned that hypothetical 10% per year on his account. At 65, Jack's retirement account was worth $596,254.

The story of Jack and Jill dramatically emphasizes the importance of starting to save and invest as early as possible. Jill invested $52,000 less than Jack, but by starting nine years sooner, had $243,000 more in her account. This is, of course, a simplification and a hypothetical situation as well. Just remember: in the real world, prices and returns go up and down almost every day, nearly on a daily basis. No security is likely to appreciate at a constant rate over an extended period of time.

Still, the point of the story holds true. Most Americans don't save enough and don't begin to save soon enough. Start now. If dollar-cost averaging is a way to implement a savings plan as you can afford it, do it. If you have savings that are not invested, invest it now, all at once—with proper asset allocation, of course. History and time are on your side.

■ CONCLUSION

Given the consistent and steady increase in the value of stocks over time, the best advice in dealing with stock markets, as always, is, "Time, not timing." Over time, stocks are a good place for your money. Why not allocate an appropriate portion of your investable money there as soon as you can? If you have a little to invest, invest what you can regularly, but if you have a lump sum to invest, history tells us to invest it sooner rather than later. Instead of trying to hedge your entry into the market with dollar-cost averaging, or flat out gambling with market timing, allocate your assets so you have an opportunity to enhance your returns and reduce your overall risk in any market conditions.

■ HELMER'S HINTS

- Don't worry about *when* to invest—create a strategy, implement it as soon as you can and stick to it.

- Dollar-cost averaging is not necessarily efficient.

- Market timing, the most popular way of trying to beat the markets by picking the right time to invest, has not proven to be effective. In fact, it is tantamount to gambling.

- Time can be your greatest ally in investing. Always remember, "Time, not timing." The proven method of enhancing returns while simultaneously reducing risk is a sound asset allocation strategy. Rather than trying to outguess the market, why not follow what history has taught us about the market? Historical performance is no guarantee of future results, but it speaks volumes to me. It seems so simple— and markets have not fundamentally changed just because they have been so good for so long.

YOUR PRETAX RETIREMENT PLAN COULD COST YOU YOUR DREAMS

The Myth: Put as much as you can into your pretax retirement plan.

The Reality: For many people, pretax retirement plans are highly inefficient.

Most people have some type of retirement plan that allows them to deduct their contributions to the plan from their income before taxes are calculated. Those plans have many names: IRA, 401(k), SEP, Keogh, 403(b) and others. Taxes on those accounts are deferred, but they are not tax-free. While they do not count against your income when earned, and any earnings on those assets are not taxed when earned either, you will have to pay taxes on those assets and earnings when they are withdrawn from the account, usually in retirement. Even your heirs will have to pay a tax when they receive the balance after you die.

Prevailing wisdom is that you should take full advantage of these plans to the extent that you are eligible to do so. In other words, everyone should invest the maximum allowed, which varies from one plan to another. Look at the reduction you can get in taxes immediately. What more do you want?

Now isn't that exactly the type of tax consequence that I encouraged you to take into consideration in Chapter 2? Well, it's certainly worth considering—but many people should reject those plans. For many, pretax retirement plans are a very bad move financially.

There, I said it. I committed blasphemy. My question to my accusers, who are many, is, "How can the same financial solution apply equally well to everyone's financial situation?" The answer is simple, "It doesn't!"

■ HOW DID WE GET HERE?

How did society get to the point where virtually everyone believes we should blindly pour our money into pretax retirement plans? To answer that question, consider who benefits if we all follow that course of action.

Contributions to these plans, by their design, and because of tax treatment, remain in place for a very long time. If you begin making contributions while you're in your 30s, you're unlikely to take any distributions until you're age 59 or later. The custodian of the money has the account for 20, 30, even 40 years. Do banks, insurance companies, mutual fund companies, brokerage houses, and other financial institutions like this arrangement? Of course they do! Think how they can accelerate that money over that length of time. Do you think they might devote some of their marketing budget to convincing investors that these accounts are good? I think it's safe to conclude that financial institutions love pretax retirement accounts and spend a great deal of money convincing the public that they should love them too.

But are they really such a great deal? Let's look at their supposed advantages.

False assumption #1: They avoid taxes. Many people tell me they participate in these plans to avoid taxes. But they don't avoid taxes at all. They simply defer taxes until that income is received. You can pay now or pay later—but you will pay.

False assumption #2: You'll be in a lower tax bracket in retirement. The assumption is that when the income is actually received and the tax on the income is due, the investor will likely be retired and in a lower tax bracket. While that may be true for people who plan to have 70% of their working income in retirement, I think you should set a higher target—as I encouraged you to do in Chapter 1. The only reason for being in a lower tax bracket in retirement is that you didn't save and plan for retirement as well as you could have.

But even the assumption that with a reduction in income you'll be in a lower tax bracket is faulty. If you're married, and together you and your spouse have combined taxable income of $70,000 per year while working, you're in the 28% federal tax bracket. Following the needs planning strategy promoted by graduates of the Eeyore School of Financial Planning, you would then strive to retire at 70% of your working income—or $49,000 a year. Now we'll check our tax tables and—whoops, that's still in the 28% federal tax bracket! By following the prevailing wisdom, you would retire with 30% less income but still be in the same tax bracket!

Furthermore, how do we know what the future tax rates will be? We don't. What we do know is that present tax rates are low when compared to the historical average. The top federal bracket as of this writing is 39.6%. Reviewing federal income tax rates back to 1913, the average top rate is about 58%. In other words, we are presently almost 20 percentage points below the historical average.

Do you trust politicians to continue to try to balance budgets or pay off our huge national debt? My suspicion is that even if budgets remain balanced, our debt won't be paid down very much. What happens then if the economy slows and revenues drop? We'll still have an enormous deficit, our national spending will probably have increased because of larger revenues in the good times—more money to spend—and we'll have shortfalls again. It's likely then that government will have to increase revenues again. And how are they likely to do it? Tax increases—the quickest way to increase revenues.

Therefore, while we don't know what future tax rates will be, we do know we presently have very low rates compared to the past and that government revenues are likely to drop when our economy slows down, as it inevitably will. Would you bet that your future tax rate will be higher or lower than it is now? My bet is higher—for all of us.

If tax rates go up, deferring tax on your pretax retirement plan will be counterproductive. Even if you are not in a higher tax bracket in the future, but retire with income in the same tax bracket that you are presently in there is very little advantage to delaying the tax.

False assumption #3: You have an immediate gain through tax deferral. Another misconception with regard to pretax retirement plans is that the tax savings are somehow available to you. For example, in a 28% federal tax bracket a $2,000 contribution to an IRA would save $560 in taxes. But that savings doesn't come to you, it's in the plan and you can't touch it without penalty—and that remains true until you reach age 59½. You can't use that money—not for your cost of living, not even for investments beyond the narrow range of equity investments that most plans offer. In truth, your spendable income has decreased by $1,440 because you had to spend $2,000 to save the $560.

If you're putting all of your investable income into your pretax retirement plan what will happen if you have a family emergency that requires you to withdraw it. You will pay a 10% penalty, plus the full amount withdrawn (even the 10% paid in penalty) will be taxed as income in the year it's withdrawn. Or what if you come up with a great idea for a business, but you need money to get it off the ground? No, you can't withdraw from your pretax retirement plan without paying the penalty. Pretax retirement plans offer almost no flexibility. They were designed for one thing only: to encourage people to create a nest egg for retirement.

The effect of some people's contributions to pretax plans is that they live like they're poor now so they won't have to live like they're poor later. That's not a very appealing trade-off, especially if other retirement planning strategies are available that may not force such a drastic choice. Sure, an effective investment strategy and retirement plan may require some sacrifices in the shorter term, but they should be balanced against an expected reward. And those sacrifices will be reduced with an effective strategy for the future.

I already told you about Phil and Lil, a couple that had good income but couldn't qualify for a home mortgage because they had more than $100,000 in credit card debt. Here's the kicker to their story: they also had more than $400,000 in 401(k) plans. Their 401(k)s were doing pretty well too, delivering a return of 12.5% a year. In other words, they were losing 3.5% a year on their pretax retirement plans, because they were paying 16% on their credit card debt! Now that's a bad investment—and a cautionary tale for those who are scraping together money for their contribution to a pretax plan. (See Chapter 12 for the happy conclusion to the Phil and Lil saga.)

■ PRETAX PLANS LOOK A LITTLE DIFFERENT IF YOU STRIKE A MATCH

There is one significant exception to my skepticism about the wisdom of pretax plans as a panacea. If your employer matches what you put into the plan, it's too good to pass up for most people—at least up to the level that your employer will match. Many employers will match your contribution up to 3% to 4% of your income. Employers who do that calculate that contribution in determining your overall compensation, so it's really part of your pay. You should make every effort to qualify for that match, because your money immediately doubles and you still get the tax deduction. Whether you contribute the maximum you are allowed, however, above any amount that your employer matches, requires careful scrutiny.

■ MY EPIPHANY— AND MY DECISION

I used to embrace the conventional wisdom on pretax retirement plans. Until about ten years ago I contributed the maximum I was allowed every year to my Keogh plan. But one day it hit me, "Why am I doing this? This money is essentially not available to me if I want to use it to start a new business, it's unavailable for lifestyle enjoyment and I really don't feel the tax advantage. I am unlikely to enjoy this money before I reach age 59½. I may not even survive until then. Isn't there a way of saving this money while simultaneously enjoying it and still getting some tax advantages?"

To make a long story short, I discontinued my contributions to my Keogh plan and invested in real estate that my family was able to enjoy immediately. The depreciation deduction on the real estate approximately equaled the tax advantage provided by my Keogh contributions. However, I was able to enjoy my money immediately instead of waiting 25 or more years.

This simplified example caused me to re-examine my entire financial philosophy. I began to challenge more conventional wisdom and, to my surprise, when I presented different ways of thinking to my clients, they also embraced them and my business flourished.

When someone tells me the rate of return on a pretax retirement plan, they usually quote the microeconomic figure, the return of the plan itself. Instead, they should be calculating the macroeconomic return, which would have to include any interest costs and lost opportunity costs because their money is tied up in pretax plans. Those costs must be deducted from the plan returns to obtain the true macroeconomic result.

■ WHO NEEDS PRETAX PLANS . . .

Pretax retirement plans do make sense for essentially three types of people, those who:

1. Have their contributions matched by their employer.

2. Are already in the highest tax brackets and have a reasonable chance of being in a lower tax bracket in retirement.

3. Those who don't have the discipline to save or invest without the plan. With all of their shortcomings for many people, pretax plans are still far better than saving and investing nothing.

■ . . . AND WHO DOESN'T.

Everyone else—but especially those who:

1. Have any outstanding consumer debt. Pay it off before you contribute to a pretax plan.

2. Are saving for a down payment on a home. Your mortgage interest deduction will probably provide a bigger tax deduction than your pretax plan even as you build equity in an asset and lock in your housing costs, which you can't do with rent.

3. Are disciplined savers and investors.

4. Invest in strategies that are tax-free, allow other tax deductions, or generate tax credits.

If you already have a pretax plan, look into the tax-advantaged strategies I mentioned in Chapter 2. They may actually offer returns competitive with your pretax plan without the limitations and drawbacks. If you find, as I think you will, that one of these options offers similar benefits, I'd suggest that you begin to direct new investments into this third "tax-advantaged file cabinet." You also must keep in mind the proper asset allocation of your investment portfolio. A primary consideration, as always, is whether your portfolio of investments is adequately diversified. Very few investors that I have met, however, have portfolios that are overweighted toward tax-advantaged strategies. The error usually comes in overweighting the second tax file cabinet: tax-deferred strategies.

■ SUMMARY OF PRETAX PLANS

Without knowing the specifics of your situation I can't say for sure whether your pretax retirement plan is the best way for you to save and invest. However I can say with certainty that pretax retirement plans:

• Do not actually avoid taxes. They merely defer taxes by deferring income.

• Provide no additional spendable income. The tax savings generated by the contribution are in the plan. In fact, spendable income actually decreases.

• Will not necessarily be taxed at a lower rate when distributed to you. We don't know what future tax rates will be. However, a compelling argument can be made for the fact that they are unlikely to be lower than they are now.

- Are heavily promoted by large financial institutions that benefit greatly by holding your money for a few decades.
- Are inefficient to die with because the beneficiary is also fully taxed.
- Do not meet the needs of many investors.

A review of the various pretax retirement plans is provided in Chapter 10: A Quick Guide to Investments. I suggest that those of you who own closely held corporations pay particular attention to the Investor Profile of Dr. Feelgood in Chapter 12, which includes reference to plans under 419A(f)(6). While the IRS may put an end to these plans, as of September 2000 they still provide an excellent vehicle for some people to reduce their taxable income.

■ WHAT DOES MAKE SENSE IN YOUR PRETAX PLAN? (MYTH ALERT!!)

If you do have a pretax plan, what should you do with it? I recommend that you go against the grain again, that you stand up to the myth that variable annuities are best as a replacement for taxable investments. I think variable annuities are excellent in a *pretax* plan. Ouch! People are throwing bricks at me again!

Once again, conventional wisdom

likes the delay of taxes that variable annuities provide for investment earnings. But this position runs into the same argument I make against pretax plans: some investors will be taxed at the same or a higher rate in the future. Furthermore, distributions from variable annuities are taxed as ordinary income—at rates as high as 39.6%—rather than at the more favorable long-term capital gains rate, which can be as low as 10%. Therefore, many investors should shy away from variable annuities for after-tax dollars, and instead consider them for pretax plans. (A description of variable annuities is also provided in Chapter 10.)

Some people might say Helmer's lost it. Why, they would ask, put pretax dollars into a variable annuity since the money is already tax-deferred and variable annuity management fees are higher than mutual fund fees? Isn't that like wearing a belt and suspenders at the same time? (Sorry to bring my Dad into this!) What traditionalists fail to address are the benefits that the investor receives in the variable annuity for the extra fees.

When traditionalists discuss fees, they do not generally consider the various pricing structures of mutual funds, funds in managed asset allocations, and variable annuities.

According to Lipper, Inc. the average no-load domestic equity mutual fund annual expense is 1.146% for the last five years. Since most variable annuities are sold through registered representatives, comparing a product that comes through an adviser to one acquired directly is not completely accurate. The adviser should be providing services beyond merely acquiring investment vehicles—and if they are not, perhaps you should look for a new adviser anyway.

However, no-load mutual funds can be purchased through a registered investment adviser for a fee. If we use an assumption that this fee is 1% to 1.5% annually, the total annual expense of a no-load domestic equity mutual fund through an adviser in a managed allocation would be around 2.15% to 2.65%.

Of the other types of mutual fund pricing structures sold through registered representatives, the one most like an annuity is a "B" share, which usually has a "back-end" load, a fee charged upon redemption. According to Lipper, Inc. the average domestic equity back-end load mutual fund has annual expenses of 2.044%. If we assumed the variable annuity acquired through registered representatives has policy-based charges (mortality and administrative expenses) of around 1.4% and expenses for domestic equity portfolios of around .8% to 1%, the total annual expenses would be approximately 2.2%-2.4%.

If fees were the only issue, variable annuities have a slight cost disadvantage to mutual funds. However, price is only a consideration in the absence of value. If price were the only factor consumers considered, we would all drive the lowest priced car, buy generic brand food, shampoo, toothpaste and other

groceries, and live in studio apartments. I did all those things when I was in college, so I know there are significant differences between the cheapest stuff and higher-quality goods.

Variable annuities offer features and benefits generally not available with a mutual fund that justify a higher cost. These features and benefits include:

- Medical waivers. Many variable annuities provide individuals with access to their funds free of any surrender charges if certain medical emergencies occur, such as terminal illness or nursing home confinement. Back-end loaded mutual funds may not provide the liquidity needed in these crucial situations.

- Simplicity of distributions. Some variable annuities will guarantee the accuracy of mandatory distributions at age 70 or early distributions prior to 59 via IRC section 72(t). I am aware of no mutual fund that makes such an offer. This service may lift a tremendous burden of responsibility from the investor. Significant penalties may apply if mandatory distributions are not taken in accordance with the law.

- Portfolio advantages: tax implications. The tax status of variable annuities gives significant advantages to the managers of variable annuity subaccounts—the investment choices an annuity holder has within the annuity. It's like a collection of mutual funds with various investment objectives. The managers of variable annuity subaccounts do not have to worry about the tax implications of their decisions for their shareholders, because all investments are on a tax-deferred basis. Managers of regular mutual funds, which may include tax-deferred investments from some, but investments from others that are currently taxable, are sometimes constrained from selling stocks when they would like to because the capital gains would have a negative impact on shareholders whose investment gains are taxable. Capital gains on stocks sold by mutual funds have to be divided among shareholders of the fund. The unfortunate possibility is that capital gains distributions could result in a tax liability for shareholders even if a fund has actually lost money in a given year! That does not make shareholders happy. As a result, fund managers may have to sell highly appreciated stock gradually over time to soften the capital gains blow to shareholders. Managers of variable annuity subaccounts don't have that headache; they can buy and sell based only on the merits of a stock.

• Portfolio advantages: cash flows. Variable annuity subaccounts are likely to have more predictable cash flows than mutual funds, which also makes the manager's job easier. Redemptions from a mutual fund can dampen the performance of that fund by forcing fund managers to sell stocks when they may not want to just to raise the cash to redeem shares. It's natural that when markets aren't performing well, investors want out. If enough investors want their money back, managers may have to sell stocks at exactly the wrong time—when prices are depressed—which hurts the performance of the fund. Since many variable annuity subaccounts have generally experienced positive cash flows and may have surrender charges, many managers have grown to like the steady consistency of managing variable annuity assets. In fact, recently published performance numbers by Lipper, Inc. have indicated superior performance from variable annuity subaccounts versus the retail mutual fund managed by the same person.

• Multiple money managers. Diversification among money managers and between fund families allows investors to take advantage of different investment styles. Some portfolios are managed like a loaded mutual fund, some like no-load mutual funds and others like institutional accounts generally not available for purchase by retail investors. Variable annuities, which bring different managers and styles together, allow the investor to structure a portfolio within the annuity to meet their needs and objectives within a single investment. The ability to properly diversify and create negative correlation has the potential to enhance performance and reduce risk exposure. Furthermore, automatic rebalancing is easily accomplished within a variable annuity even if the money is allocated among various managers and subaccounts. This could be expensive and cumbersome, if an investor simply held a variety of mutual funds outside a variable annuity.

- Guaranteed death benefit. Most variable annuities have a guaranteed death benefit. It means that investors are guaranteed a certain return on their money, usually 5% to 7%, if their account had not performed up to that level when they die. This "die in a down market clause" may also provide investors with the confidence to invest in equities without as much concern about how market fluctuations will affect their beneficiaries, choosing more aggressive long-term asset allocations in an effort to earn the higher returns that equities have historically provided. This benefit alone, in my opinion, is worth the extra cost for most investors.

■ VALUE FOR DOLLARS SPENT

Those who bash variable annuities are many. But their opposition focuses on cost—and they overstate the difference in cost without apparently understanding the additional benefits being purchased.

For instance, one author who is critical of variable annuities contends that less than 1% of people ever die in a down market and therefore do not utilize that provision of a variable annuity contract. The author concludes that since so few people benefit from this provision it is essentially worthless. Would that author also recommend that people drop their homeowners insurance just because so few people ever have a claim?

You may own your home and I would presume that if you do you have homeowners insurance. If you are not lucky enough to have your house burn down or blow away in a tornado, is your homeowners insurance a waste of money? The fact that you haven't filed a claim doesn't diminish the importance of protecting your home. Try canceling your policy and see how well you sleep. The variable annuity death benefit is like equity portfolio insurance and you need not die in a down market for it to have value.

Having the security of that benefit can be like a permission slip to continue to invest aggressively in equities even as you get older and your time horizon gets shorter. You can ignore the prevailing wisdom of getting out of stocks as you get older. Divesting your stock portfolio may reduce your risk exposure but it is also possible that it will reduce your investment performance. However, with portfolio insurance you establish a "floor" for your investment performance and can remain invested. It also has the potential to enhance your performance. In my experience, the potential for higher return on investment more than covers the slight extra cost paid for the benefit.

Just a reminder: Both mutual funds and variable annuity investment sub-accounts involve market risk, including fluctuating returns and possible loss of principal. In addition, early withdrawals from variable annuities may involve additional fees and tax penalties.

■ CONCLUSION

Pretax retirement plans were created to encourage average people to save and invest. But they have been embraced far too widely—in many cases by people who don't need them. Sure you get a tax break now, but that money is locked up until you are 59½ years old unless you're willing to pay a steep penalty for premature withdrawals. You can't invest it in yourself, you can't invest it in a home (in most cases), and you can't enjoy it. The last straw is that you may be deferring taxes on that income until you are in a *higher* tax bracket. Tax-deferred plans are a good part of an investment plan, but they certainly shouldn't be all of it. Remember, you want money in all three tax file cabinets: taxable, tax-deferred, and tax-advantaged.

If your employer matches your contribution, put in as much as will be matched. Take any other income you would be permitted to invest in a pretax plan and investigate tax-advantaged investments that could be much more efficient in the long run. If your employer doesn't match your contribution, I'd recommend stopping your contributions until you have your finances in better balance—especially if your pretax plan is your only investment or savings vehicle.

I would also encourage you to look into the benefits of adding a variable annuity to your tax-deferred plan. You'll pay slightly higher management fees, and your access to the money will be more restricted, but the advantages may more than compensate for those fees.

■ HELMER'S HINTS

- Pretax plans are not the panacea for investing that the fund companies would have you believe— but they get to hold your money for decades, don't they?

- Contribute what your employer will match. After that, begin shifting your savings or assets into tax-*advantaged* rather than just tax-*deferred* investments.

- The best tax reduction strategy you can use, and probably the most enjoyable for you and your family, is to purchase a home.

LIFE INSURANCE ISN'T JUST FOR DYING

7

The Myth: Life insurance is a bad investment.

The Reality: Life insurance provides investment opportunities that address multiple issues simultaneously: protection, appreciation, income taxes, and estate taxes.

Life insurance can be an excellent investment—even if you don't die for a very long time. As I start to write this chapter I can already imagine the blood pressure rising in a lot of financial gurus as they leap to their feet to object. "Life insurance as an investment vehicle? Are you kidding me?"

You're probably thinking the same thing—because that's what nearly everybody thinks. Well, not me. And not dozens and dozens of my clients who are quite happy they followed my advice instead of conventional wisdom on this topic.

Let's begin at the point where most people get stuck when it comes to considering life insurance. They ask, "How much do I need?" Uh-oh. Bad start! They've already turned down the wrong road—and they won't get far.

■ DO YOU NEED IT OR WANT IT?

When people ask me how much life insurance they need, I tell them that life insurance isn't a need product, it's a *want* product, a love product. If I die before my wife and kids, I want them to have as much money as possible in my absence. Sometimes people question whether children can be spoiled by too much money. I don't believe anyone can have too much money—only too little character.

Why do people get hung up by looking at life insurance as a need?

First, most people aren't willing to face death, so it's hard to convince them that they really do *need* life insurance. None of us wants to consider the prospect that we will die soon; if we do consider the prospect, we dismiss it as very remote. Chances are, however, that you currently have auto and homeowner's insurance. You may also be insured for health care, disability income, and liability risks. But you may never even file a claim on any of these policies. You may never sustain damage to your home, for example, but you cannot afford not to cover that risk. However, we all die someday. Death is inevitable. Why do we insure assets with less value than our lives against risks that may never occur and yet we choose not to insure a risk that is certain—death—for a far more valuable asset—our lives?

Second, when people try to figure out how much life insurance they need, they tend to become immobilized and do nothing.

How do you calculate your life insurance needs anyway? How do you know what your family's needs will be in an indefinite future? VCRs, cellular phones, home computers, and the Internet are just a few examples of things that did not even exist a few short years ago. How could you have planned for needs that did not exist in even the recent past?

Is homeowner's insurance a need product? Let's think about that. Assume you own a home worth $200,000. Does your policy cover the entire $200,000 value? Consider the following scenarios:

- You have $50,000 cash in the bank, which you could access if your house were destroyed and you needed to rebuild. So, would you insure your home for only $150,000?

- You *want* that $200,000 home but really only *need* a home that costs about $125,000. Would you insure your home for only $125,000?

- You have a lake cabin worth $75,000. Nobody *needs* a lake cabin. So, since it's something you only *want* but don't *need*, you probably wouldn't insure your cabin at all, right?

Don't these examples sound silly?

Obviously you would insure these assets for what they're worth. That's why we have insurance: to replace things of value. Would it not then follow that you would also insure your life for what it's worth to your family? Most Americans don't. They have been told by nearly everyone that life insurance beyond some minimal level is a waste of money.

The third problem with a focus on need is that most of us are motivated more by what we want than by what we need—especially when that need does not seem urgent. Instead, we spend our money on what we want today.

Sometimes people don't do what's good for them even as they acknowledge that it would be good for them. Consider the case of my clients, Jan and Gary. About three years ago, as part of a complete plan, I advised Jan and Gary to buy variable universal life (VUL) insurance contracts on themselves. There were two very good reasons for them to be motivated to follow my advice. First, they had small children and a mortgage, so if either of them died, the survivor would face severe financial hardship. Second, Jan and Gary were in their early 30s; since the cost would be relatively low, the VUL would be an excellent long-term investment strategy.

They agreed that the VULs made sense. However, here we are three years later and they still haven't taken any action on the VUL policies. Every time I remind them, they tell me they like the idea but just don't have the cash flow right now, but they soon will. Then, they'll buy the VUL contracts.

Their reasoning doesn't work for me, however, because I know that both Jan and Gary participate in their company 401(k) plans. I consider the VUL a better alternative for them at this point than the 401(k). Furthermore, they recently went out and bought a new boat. Obviously, I would consider the VULs to be more important than a boat.

Why haven't Jan and Gary invested in VULs? My guess is that they see the VULs as something they need as opposed to something they really want. We are all more motivated by our wants than by our needs. Sound silly? Would you rather spend your money on medicine or a nice juicy steak? A lawnmower or a snowmobile? Sensible shoes or a new dress?

Even though Jan and Gary feel that they ought to have the VULs, it hasn't been a priority, because they don't truly want them. Don't misunderstand my point: I'm not against boats or enjoying life. Maybe it's my fault for not demonstrating effectively enough why they should really *want* the VULs.

I had advised Jan and Gary to contribute $500 a month to the VUL strategy. If they funded the VUL for 30 years at a hypothetical net tax-free yield of 8%, their account would grow to $734,075. However, if they were to start today, just three years later, and invested the same amount and earned the same return for 27 instead of 30 years, the account value would be only $566,033. Accounting for the $18,000

reduction in their contributions over that time, Jan and Gary's cost of waiting only three years has been $150,042. You could buy a heck of a nice boat for that. I'm not sure how I could have made it any clearer than this.

As long as they treat it as a need product, people tend to view life insurance as something they'll do tomorrow or they view it as a need to meet at minimum and then move on.

Those people are missing an important financial opportunity. This is about where I begin to get angry. Life insurance is so misunderstood, even by the financial masters, that it's no wonder people raise their eyebrows when I recommend it.

Why do I recommend it? Because it's the most efficient way to ensure the financial security of your family. Is it a waste of money? Only if you do it the way people in the financial industry— even the insurance companies—recommend that you do it. But if you do it the right way, life insurance provides protection for your family, very attractive appreciation potential, significant tax benefits, and financial flexibility like no other financial products. For those reasons, nearly everyone should *want* life insurance even if they plan to defy mortality.

But it's tough to convince people of those advantages. So, before we get into the reasons why you would want life insurance in your investment universe, let's back up a minute and look at how we got to the point where life insurance as an investment is so reviled.

GIVING MONEY TO INSURANCE COMPANIES: TERM VS. PERM

For years the debate has raged. Which is more efficient—buying permanent life insurance or buying term insurance and investing the cost difference?

A term insurance policy provides a fixed sum of death benefit for a fixed length of time, usually 20-30 years. The policy is priced according to the statistical likelihood of the death of the person insured. If you're young and healthy, you can buy term insurance very cheaply, because the odds are against you dying during the term the insurance is in force. If you're old and sick, the cost is very, very high, because it's much more likely that the insurance company will have to pay.

Permanent life insurance (PLI or perm) is a policy that pays a predetermined death benefit for which you pay a set premium for your life. It covers your life not for a set period of time, or term, but until you actually die. Because the permanent policy will almost certainly pay a death benefit at some time—most all of us die!—it's naturally more expensive. The payments for that insurance are spread out over your expected life.

The higher premiums are the cause for the debate about whether to buy perm or settle for term and invest the difference in premiums in other assets.

A lot of powerful interests have a stake in whether you buy term or perm and all of them—including the life insurance companies themselves!—would prefer that you buy term insurance.

It's easy to see why the brokerages, mutual fund companies, and banks would prefer that you buy term. If you buy term and invest the difference, where will you put that money? Of course, you'll avail yourself of the services of these institutions. You'll invest your money with them, probably for a very long time. They get the money, not the insurance companies. (One of the catches to the term and perm debate, however, is that many people don't actually invest the difference in premiums; they spend it. But enough invest it that it's in the interests of Wall Street to advocate term insurance and hope to get your money.)

But why would insurance companies prefer to sell term insurance if they get more money up front by selling perm? The answer can be found in a study done at Penn State University, which concluded that fewer than one term policy in six survives to the end of the term for which it was written and less than 1% of all term insurance policies *ever* pay a death claim.[6] That means that most people who buy term insurance quit paying the premiums before the term ends and a very low percentage of policies result in claims paid. Since they seldom pay a death claim, one can rea-

---

6 "Some Empirical Observations on Term Life Insurance: Revisited,"Arthur L. Williams, *The Journal of Insurance Issues and Practices,* January 1984.

sonably assume that insurance companies love to issue term insurance. The money goes only one way, into the insurance companies' coffers.

Life insurance companies know that, but most people who buy term life insurance don't consider it. But that's one big reason that term insurance is a very inefficient use of your money—even apart from the other advantages of perm insurance, which I'll discuss in a minute.

Remember our discussion of opportunity cost? We learned that whenever there's a cost in our financial world, we have not only that cost, but also the cost of not being able to use that money to earn a return. When you add the cost of lost opportunity to the cost of premiums, term insurance is not nearly as cheap as you might think.

Assume a 35-year-old male pays $360 per year for $250,000 in term death benefit coverage for 30 years. That $360 earns nothing. If we assume he earns a hypothetical 10% annual return on that money if he invests it, the actual cost of his insurance over 30 years, assuming premiums *never* go up, is not just $10,800 ($360 x 30 years), but $65,140 ($360 x 30 years compounding at 10%). Furthermore, if he then drops the coverage at age 65, because it's become cost-prohibitive and he doesn't really need it anymore, the opportunity cost still continues through the rest of his life (14 more years, statistically). Therefore, the total cost is $247,369! ($65,140 x 14 years compounding at 10%) In the final analysis, $250,000 of death benefit costs

nearly $250,000, but he drops the coverage before he can collect—at an age when statistically he is more likely to die! Of course, this entire scenario is very unlikely because, according to the Penn State study, there is less than a 1% chance that this person would actually pay the premium for 30 years.

So you are very unlikely to get any benefit from buying term insurance—ever! But is perm any better?

■ RENTING VS. OWNING

You are probably currently making mortgage payments. If you're renting instead, you perhaps plan to buy a home someday. You can probably rent for a lower monthly cost than a mortgage payment. So why not continue to rent? There are probably many reasons you are willing to pay more to buy a home (remember: cost is an issue only in the absence of value), but one primary reason is because you will *own* the home. You build equity with your mortgage payment. With rent, the money all goes down the drain. You ultimately move and get nothing back from all your rent payments.

Term is comparable to renting, while permanent is comparable to owning. Your payments for permanent insurance give you something with tangible value, just like owning real estate. Perm is an asset. It has cash value and a death benefit for life. With term there is a greater than 99% chance you won't even make your rent payments to the end of the lease—and you won't get any money back anyway.

■ PERMANENT CHANGES FOR THE BETTER

The problem with permanent life insurance, if you go back a couple of decades to the time when many of us learned about finances from our parents, was that the returns you could earn on the money invested in perm insurance, above the cost of the death benefit, were very conservative. You probably had a good opportunity to do better investing the difference in premiums yourself, because the cash value of the life insurance was invested in fixed-interest investments that provided a low return.

The returns on permanent life insurance changed dramatically, however, when a new type of permanent life insurance was created in the late 1970s—variable universal life insurance.

With a VUL, the cash value of life insurance is invested in equity portfolios wrapped inside the life insurance. The internal mutual fund-like accounts are called subaccounts and can be compared to retail mutual funds. Insurance subaccounts, in fact, are often managed by the same managers who manage retail mutual funds. The performance is likely to be comparable, except for two major differences:

- The earnings of a retail mutual fund are taxable (unless owned inside some type of pretax retirement plan), while earnings in a VUL are not.
- The VUL deducts life insurance costs.

However, the performance of VUL subaccounts often exceeds that of retail funds because the managers don't have to be concerned about tax liabilities for shareholders. That improved performance often makes up for some of the insurance cost. With access to typical market returns on investment, the VUL offers the potential of significantly better performance than earlier life insurance investments provided. This innovation eliminated one of the major objections to permanent life insurance—that it was a bad investment. For investors who are middle-aged or younger, and in a moderate tax bracket, it is possible that a VUL will *outperform* retail mutual funds. (Note: both mutual funds and variable annuity investment sub-accounts involve market risk, including fluctuating returns and possible loss of principal. In addition, early withdrawals from and loans taken against VULs may involve additional fees and tax penalties and may negatively affect death benefits.)

With the advent of the VUL, you could buy life insurance that would almost certainly pay a benefit someday (unlike term insurance) and has the potential to earn competitive returns. But the advantages don't end there. You'll understand why you should truly *want* life insurance as an investment vehicle, however, when we look at the strategic applications of life insurance.

■ STRATEGIC APPLICATIONS OF PERMANENT LIFE INSURANCE

The current tax advantages of life insurance can make it an attractive investment strategy even if you have no desire (or need) for the death benefit. There is a drag on the internal rate of return for the costs unique to life insurance, primarily for the death benefit. However, depending on your age, sex, health, and tax bracket, the tax advantages of life insurance may more than offset the internal costs.

The higher the tax bracket, the greater the advantages. The greatest advantages also will be enjoyed by people who are young and healthy, because the mortality cost of the insurance (the amount you pay for the death benefit) is lower for those who are not likely to die for a long time. Women also enjoy some advantages in the cost of life insurance, because statistically they live longer. So, the ideal candidate for a permanent life insurance policy is a young, healthy, affluent woman.

In my experience, permanent life insurance is almost certain to be advantageous for healthy people up until the age of 50. After that age, health becomes a critical factor in determining the potential benefits. Permanent life insurance is seldom a good strategy for people over the age of 65, because the mortality cost of the insurance would be too high.

The often-overlooked strategic advantage of permanent life insurance in a financial plan is that it can be used as a conduit to other investment strategies. New money goes into perm, which then serves as a "holding tank." We can take distributions from our holding tank for personal use—such as to pay for college or start a new business—or invest in assets not available through the insurance subaccounts—such as a "can't miss" stock or real estate. We can even take distributions and reinvest them in pretax plans or a Roth IRA if we want to.

If we have taxable earnings on our new investment, those earnings can then be directed back into the insurance policy and not allowed to compound, an acceleration strategy we discussed in Chapter 3. Using perm insurance as the conduit to other investments is an effective way to potentially increase benefits and earnings, because no new money is wasted by first going into assets that do not produce benefits. Perm insurance does not replace other investments and is not necessarily better than other investments. But, it enhances those other investments by making them more efficient.

Let's assume you contribute $5,000 a year to a permanent life insurance policy for 10 years. Therefore, you have a basis of $50,000. However, there is $100,000 of equity (cash value) in the contract. Because the policy has the unique accounting treatment of first-in-first-out (FIFO), you could withdraw $50,000 and not trigger a tax liability because the withdrawal is treated as a return of basis. However, if you withdrew the entire $100,000, you would receive a 1099 for the $50,000 gain and that gain would be taxed at ordinary income tax rates. The way to avoid the income tax, if you desire a distribution that exceeds your basis, is to take out a loan from the insurance company, with your policy as collateral.

Most permanent life insurance contracts offer a very low net cost to borrow money against the cash value of your policy. Unlike a withdrawal, a policy loan does not disturb the contract's equity: the company actually lends you money and the equity in the contract serves as collateral. An amount equal to the loan is set aside and credited with an interest rate generally in a range from 2% to 4% below to the same as the interest rate you are being charged to borrow. In other words, generally the worst case is a 4% net cost, but some contracts even allow for zero cost loans!

Now, here's where things get interesting. Assume you are able to have a zero cost loan: the insurance company charges you 6% and internally credits back the same 6% on the same dollar value as the loan. You would still have a statement showing the interest cost, which is effectively a phantom number because you earned the same interest within the contract equity.

Further assume you get the loan in order to reinvest. If you borrow $10,000 at 6%, you get a statement showing a $600 interest cost after a year. (You also simultaneously earned $600 in the contract.) You reinvest the $10,000 somewhere that earns a hypothetical 12%, generating a 1099 showing $1,200 in taxable earnings. As we learned in the discussion of the acceleration of money, it would be a good idea for you to put the $1,200 of earnings back into the insurance contract so your tax liability doesn't compound. Under current tax laws, the $600 interest cost is deductible against the $1,200 of investment income, thus creating yet another tax advantage.

So, not only did the contract allow for a tax-free distribution, but it also allowed for a deduction against portfolio earnings! If you use the proceeds of a policy loan for investment or business purposes, and you can prove that use, the interest on the loan is usually deductible. You can do this not just once, but as often as you would like. Dollars go into the insurance account, then are repositioned to other investments, then back into insurance repeatedly, thus increasing the acceleration of money.

Moreover, the earnings in your insurance contract are in most cases income tax free—and unlike a traditional IRA those earnings may be income tax free to your heirs, an enormous advantage over investing the money yourself, even if the taxes are deferred.

■ THE THREE LITTLE PIGS

You're probably familiar with the story of the three little pigs. But, you probably do not know what happened to them after they escaped that wolf in the third pig's house of bricks.

The three little pigs continued to live and work together. They all became independent corn tasters at corn canning and processing plants. They greatly enjoyed their jobs and prospered equally. Each of the three pigs earned about $60,000 per year, which put them all in a combined state and federal tax bracket of 35%. Also, they all determined to invest about 10% of their annual incomes.

The first little pig, the genius that built the straw house, started to save $500 dollars per month at age 45 (in pig years). He put his $500 per month into a nice portfolio of taxable mutual funds that earned 10% per year. By age 60, when he retired, he had accumulated $150,127 in his portfolio after taxes.

The second little pig, the one that had lived in the stick house, also started saving at age 45 and he put $500 per month into a tax-deferred portfolio that earned 9% per year. By age 60 he had accumulated $184,641. Of course, upon beginning any distributions he would have to pay the taxes that he had been deferring while accumulating the money.

The third little pig, he of brick house fame, like his brothers began saving $500 per month at age 45. He invested in a tax-advantaged plan that earned 9%. By age 60 he had accumulated $162,207.

You're probably wondering how pig 2 invested the same amount, over the same 15 years, and earned the same 9% but by age 60 had accumulated an additional $22,434. That's because the third little pig's tax-advantaged investment strategy was a variable universal life insurance policy. His return was lower due to his insurance cost. Ouch! Seems

like a bad deal so far—but let's look at the impact on their retirement years.

At age 60, each of the three pigs decided he needed $1,000 dollars per month in his 35% tax bracket to support his lifestyle in retirement. The first little pig needed to withdraw $16,671 per year to net that $12,000. The second little pig needed to withdraw $18,462 from his tax-deferred account per year to net $12,000. (Because the first little pig had invested after-tax dollars, some of the value of his account was his basis, which could not be taxed again. Since he owed less tax on what he withdrew than the second pig, he did not need to withdraw as much to net $12,000.) The third little pig was able to take $12,000 per year in distributions with no tax liability.

Unfortunately, the first pig ran out of money at age 82. Even though he continued to earn 10% on his investments, the annual distribution of $16,671 wore the account down to nothing in 22 years. The second little pig had only $9,201 left at age 82, so he would run out of money six months later. However, the third little pig still had $219,271 in his account. Not only had he not run out of money like pigs one and two, but his account had actually grown by more than $57,000. In fact, when he died at age 95, the third little pig's *tax-advantaged* account was worth $231,889: it had kept him living comfortably—and grown another $12,618 after he turned 82.

Figure 7.1 summarizes the experiences of the three little pigs. Each started saving $500 a month at age 45 and retired at age 60. The first little pig earned 10% a year on his savings in a taxable account. The second little pig earned 9% a year in a tax-deferred account. The third little pig earned 9% a year in a tax-advantaged account—a variable universal life insurance policy. Each little pig was in a combined federal and state tax bracket of 35%.

Let's take a closer look at the results of the third little pig's investment strat-

him in his encounter with the wolf. Just as his investment in a brick house kept him safe from the wolf at his door, his investment of $500 per month in a variable universal life insurance policy put him far ahead in his later years. Oh, by the way, the third little pig did not *need* the life insurance. He *wanted* it.

Which Investment Strategy Would You Copy?

	1st Pig	2nd Pig	3rd Pig
Account at age 60	$150,127	$184,641	$162,207
Annual Withdrawal to Net $12,000	16,671	18,462	12,000
Account at age 80	12,810	32,243	212,481
Account at age 82	0	9,201	219,271
Account at age 95	0	0	231,889

Figure 7.1

egy. He invested $6,000 per year for 15 years for a total investment of $90,000. He received distributions of $12,000 per year for 35 years, totaling $420,000. When he died he still had $231,889 in his account. Think about this a moment. He invested $90,000 and received $420,000 in his golden years and then left another $281,889 income tax-free to his heirs! Are you impressed by this investment strategy? I think you should be.

Whose investment strategy would you copy? We knew that third little pig was smart from the time we first met

■ TWO MORE INSURANCE RECOMMENDATIONS

Before we leave the subject of insurance, I want you to think about two other types of insurance that could play a significant role in your financial future. One type nearly everyone truly needs: disability insurance. The other is not needed by the wealthiest or the poorest people, but should be considered by everyone else when they're in their 50s: long-term care insurance.

■ DISABILITY INSURANCE: INSURANCE YOU NEED WHETHER YOU WANT IT OR NOT

One of the most important types of insurance is disability income (DI). Yet most people don't appreciate its value. Only about 40% of workers in the United States are estimated to have DI.[7]

Why do you need disability insurance? Well, what is your largest asset? Your house, your car, your company pension plan? If you're still working, your most significant asset is probably your ability to produce income.

How important is disability income insurance? Consider the following fact: If you are between the ages of 35 and 65, your odds of suffering a disability that lasts 90 days are about 30%.[8] You are more likely to suffer a disability than a serious loss on your home. Yet, although nearly everyone carries homeowner's insurance, most of us roll the dice and take our chances when it comes to disability income coverage.

One of the primary reasons people avoid disability insurance is the cost. Annual premiums will typically range between 2% and 3% of your salary.[9] As with all types of insurance, the cheaper the policy premium, the more *un*likely that the insurance company will ever need to pay a claim. Conversely, when the policy is expensive, there's usually a higher probability that the policy

owner will file a claim. You can infer from this that the more expensive the policy, the more likely you'll benefit from the protection!

Most people with disability coverage have it because their employer provides it. But this type of coverage—group disability—has several problems:

- If you leave the company, the coverage ends.

- Employers can control the cost of the coverage and even cancel coverage if they so choose.

- Group policies can have a very restrictive definition of "disability."

- If you become disabled, your benefit from a group plan is treated as taxable income if your employer paid the premium. If you fund your own policy, on the other hand, you receive the disability benefits tax-free.

It can be difficult to get the appropriate amount of disability coverage. This is particularly true for those who are self-employed. Disability companies need to know how much income the applicant has earned over the past two years. If you recently started your own company, you don't have two years' history of income. It doesn't matter if you think you will earn significantly more than you made working for someone else, disability companies don't like

---

[7] "The Big Risk That Few Workers Protect Against," *The New York Times,* February 6, 2000.
[8] Ibid.
[9] Ibid.

newly self-employed people, who tend to have volatile incomes. Disability companies want to base their coverage on a consistent income.

In spite of the difficulties of applying for disability income coverage and in spite of the cost, most people should have disability insurance. The cost of not having this important coverage and suffering a disability is simply too great a risk. Get it!

■ LONG-TERM CARE INSURANCE: IF YOU'RE IN THE MIDDLE, YOU'D BETTER CHECK IT OUT

Long-term care insurance protects your assets in the event that you need an extended stay in a nursing home facility or some other long-term health care. It's essentially disability income insurance for retirees.

The need for long-term care is a relatively recent phenomenon, because people are living longer than ever. Around the turn of the last century, the average life expectancy was 46 or 47 years. Today, Americans are living beyond age 76, thanks primarily to advances in medicine and health care.

Consider the following facts:[10]

- The national annual average cost for a nursing home stay is nearly $50,000.

- About 22% of people over age 85 are in a nursing home.

- 7 million people over the age of 65 will need some type of long-term care this year.

How long will you be able to pay for a nursing home for you or your spouse before you spend yourself down to the poverty level? Will you be like the many who tell a nursing home admissions officer, "I never thought I'd live this long?"

Here are the two key questions: Who needs long-term care, and how do you pay for it?

If you earn from your assets more than the $50,000 average annual cost of nursing home care, then extended health care expenses would probably not deplete your assets and long-term care may not be a financial concern for you. But, even if you can afford to pay your own bills if you need to, there's still a compelling argument for obtaining long-term care insurance. Do wealthy people cancel their auto and homeowners insurance simply because they can afford a new home or car? No. Why should health care be any different?

On the flip side, if you have very few assets to protect, you also probably do not need long-term care—and can't afford it anyway. People with lower incomes are eligible for Medicaid and not required to pay the costs themselves.

However, most people are in the middle, between these two groups, and would be excellent candidates for long-term care coverage. Long-term care can be a crisis for the middle class.

---

[10] Estimates provided by Health Industry Association of America.

The most efficient time to purchase long-term care insurance is probably when you are in your 50s. Although it's unlikely that you'll need it for some time, it's much cheaper than if you wait until you are over age 60. Also, from a health standpoint, you're far more likely to qualify for coverage. If you are over 70 and just starting to consider long-term care, it's probably too late and the cost likely will be prohibitive.

Some key features to look for in a long-term care policy include:

- Coverage of at least $100 per day
- Inflation protection
- Coverage not limited to skilled nursing homes
- No prior hospitalization required
- The ability to stop paying premiums once you've received benefits for 90 days
- Coverage for home health care

The primary advantage of long-term care insurance is that it's the most effective way to protect your estate from being depleted by health care costs. If protecting your estate is not a concern, you don't need it: the premiums are too high.

■ CONCLUSION

Contrary to the advice of many financial "experts"—including those from many life insurance companies—I believe that most people will have a very successful financial plan if they put a significant portion of their new money into permanent life insurance. With the advent of variable universal life insurance, you have the potential to achieve competitive returns on the money you invest in life insurance. You may not have the most money that you possibly could, but you would have the opportunity for financial independence.

Permanent life insurance enables you to avoid many of the negative myths about your financial future and take advantage of many of the realities we've discussed. It will help you avoid the popular and misguided overreliance on pretax retirement plans. It will help you avoid some of the opportunity cost of term insurance. It will give you a holding tank or "bucket of money" from which to reposition investments so you can accelerate your money, instead of letting your tax liability compound.

Term insurance may be an economic necessity for people with dependents. Many people do not have the financial resources to purchase as much death benefit as they would like to protect their family on a permanent basis. It's better to get enough insurance to properly protect your loved ones rather than get less death benefit permanently. But, term is not more efficient. Permanent life insurance is far more efficient. If you acquire term due to economic necessity, you should convert it to permanent as quickly as your economic situation will allow.

Disability insurance is a necessity. Too few people have protection against a disruption in their ability to earn a living—a more common occurrence than most people realize. It protects your greatest asset: your ability to earn the money upon which the rest of your financial plan is based.

Long-term care insurance may be a valuable investment if you're able to afford it and need to protect your assets and if you're not wealthy enough to cover the high expenses of extended health care.

■ HELMER'S HINTS

- Look at life insurance through the glass of *want* instead of just *need* and you'll see some very attractive reasons for acquiring it—instead of a new boat, perhaps.

- Life insurance has changed dramatically in the last couple decades. Potential returns on permanent life insurance policies are not what they were in your parent's day. What made sense to them back then may not make sense to you now. Examining your financial future through the prism of the past may make you susceptible to many myths of financial planning.

- Get disability insurance! It covers one of the greatest variables in any financial plan—future income and the potential loss of that income.

LISTEN TO THE PROS
INSTEAD OF THE CONS

8

The Myth: Hiring a financial planner is a waste of your money.

The Reality: Buying the services of a good financial planner could be one of your best investments.

Do you really need a financial planner? Of course, I would recommend that you use the services of a professional, but I'm biased. I think I add value to my clients' plans and the execution of those plans. If I didn't think I did, I'd get out of the business.

I've been in the business about 18 years. I believe myself to be of above average intelligence. Despite being reasonably bright and dedicating years of my life to the study of personal finance, as any listener to my radio show knows, I frequently do not know the answer to personal finance questions. Therefore, it's reasonable to assume that almost all consumers do not have all the answers either. In fact, they likely don't even know how much they don't know! The more I learn in this industry, the more I realize how much I have still to learn.

Think about it. If you have leaky pipes, you probably call a plumber. If you want to sue someone or if someone

sues you, you call an attorney to represent you. If you're not feeling well and you're not sure why, you're likely to call a doctor. You probably visit a doctor for periodic checkups even if you do feel well. It does not make sense to assume that you know any more about personal finance than it does to assume that you can effectively represent yourself in a court of law.

Throughout this discussion of your financial future, I've stressed the efficiency of money to help you reach your goals and live the life you imagine. I would extend the same thinking to whether you want to create a financial plan and manage it yourself. Is that the way you want to spend your time? Is it part of the life you imagine or dream of? I hire people to do everything I can for me that I'd rather not do or I don't feel qualified to do. Of course, there are limits to what services any of us can afford to hire. I don't have a butler or a personal chef at home, even though my wife and I sometimes don't feel like cooking dinner. But we do go out to eat on some of those occasions! In my own efficiency calculations in my personal life, I have to consider the value of my time.

■ WILL YOU RECEIVE VALUE FOR YOUR MONEY?

Financial publications—such as *Money, The Wall Street Journal, Forbes, Fortune, and Smart Money*—and many financial authors have something in common. Besides the fact that reading them may be hazardous to your wealth, they place great significance on fees and costs when discussing planning and investing. Therefore, many Americans have become very cost-conscious. Being cost-conscious is good—but emphasizing cost to the detriment of value is bad. The magazines, authors, and many investors have developed a blind spot with regard to cost.

Let's look at a hypothetical investment—let's call it Fund A. (This is for illustrative purposes only and does not represent any specific investment.) Say you have owned this fund for seven years and your average annual return has been 17% net after costs. You wish you had owned Fund A longer, because over the last 20 years it has averaged about a 20% net annual return!

Fund A has a front-end load of 5.5%—which would eliminate it from the universe of investments that many gurus would have you consider. It also has annual maintenance and marketing expenses of 1.44%. Prevailing wisdom would have you avoid Fund A because its costs are high in comparison with some no-load funds that have annual maintenance fees as low as 0.3%. However, by looking at the mutual fund performances listed by Morningstar,

Inc. a company that tracks mutual fund performance, I can count on one hand the funds that have performed as well as our hypothetical Fund A over the last 20 years. In other words, the shareholders in Fund A may have paid higher costs than investors in no-load funds, but they still received good value for the costs associated with Fund A. They received good value even after costs were taken into consideration.

Of course, the costs associated with any particular fund have no correlation to its performance. Research has determined that there is no correlation between costs and performance. Load funds will not necessarily outperform no-load funds. But let's say Fund A has performed extremely well—and has more than justified the cost.

As an investor and as a financial adviser, I am less concerned with cost than with actual net dollars earned. I don't mind paying a front load and annual fees of 1.44% if my net is 20% per year for 20 years.

Cost is an issue only in the absence of value. That was a lesson I learned in college. In my senior year I had to travel 16 miles five days a week to student teach. Money was tight, so I bought a 14-year-old car with 150,000 miles on it to make the commute. Well, within a couple weeks, I had spent more in parts and repairs than I paid for the car. And there was no way to put a dollar figure on the stress and aggravation I endured wondering each day if that old car would get me to class. I couldn't function up to my level of ability because of the stress that car created. Maybe it's no wonder, in light of that experience, that I never became a teacher. The lesson for me was clear: I needed to look beyond cost and focus on the bottom line. The same thinking applies to hiring a professional to help you plan your future.

A good financial planner can add value in many ways:

- Creating additional investable capital. Many consumers have inefficient strategies in place. A good planner can suggest strategies that can free up more investable capital without detracting from one's lifestyle.

- Being objective. Many otherwise intelligent people can have a hard time being objective about their own personal finances.

- Identifying goals. A good planner can help to clarify a vision of one's future.

- Saving time. Many people are so busy with the day-to-day demands of work and family that they want to delegate responsibility for their money.

- Worrying about your money for you. Most people realize they don't have the desire, time, or aptitude to manage their own money efficiently. Therefore, they worry about it. I tell clients that it's my job to worry for them and if they are still worrying after I'm on board, maybe they should hire someone else.

Why do many of my clients hire my services? Because I'm smarter than they are? I don't believe that—and neither do they! They hire me for what I know, even though they are capable of learning what I know. It's just not how they choose to spend their time.

■ WHAT IS USUALLY OVERLOOKED IN SELF-MADE PLANS

If you devote the time and energy to it, you may be able to create your own financial plan—with one very important exception: you probably will not be able to integrate effective tax strategies into that plan even if you do consider the tax liabilities of your investments. Taxes are the big complication—but tax strategies also present an enormous opportunity to use your money more efficiently.

It's ugly, but it's a fact of life that the U.S. tax code is appalling in its complexity. Sure, some things have been done to reduce that complexity, but the effect has been to make efficient tax strategies seem that much more complicated for the average investor and taxpayer. Most consumers don't understand the laws and are forced to hire accountants and attorneys to help calculate what they need to pay. This costs Americans billions annually and distracts our country and gifted people from doing more productive things. Intelligent, gifted people spend their lives helping people pay the right tax. What a waste! Couldn't these bright people do something more constructive if the tax laws were simplified?

Many solutions to this maze have been proposed and many more will be. That's the killer. Powerful special interests will always fight to get preferential tax treatment. Congress will forever tinker with tax codes. They will always be changing. Very few people know the details of our tax code well enough to devise efficient tax-reduction strategies, and still fewer can keep up with all the changes. I'll be the first to admit that I don't know all the details. But I'm smart enough to acknowledge what I don't know. That's why my company includes accountants and a tax attorney—people whose business it is to know what's possible and what's legal.

I would strongly advise you to determine how you can reduce taxes as much as possible. Pay what you must, but pay no more. So even if you do create your own plan, hire the services of a qualified professional who can examine the tax consequences of your plan and perhaps recommend alternative strategies that will reduce your taxes.

You might think that you don't have enough assets to qualify for tax-reduction strategies, but you may be surprised at how little you need to invest to avail yourself of these opportunities—especially if you don't concentrate simply on reducing taxes *this* year. Too many people rely too heavily on tax-deferred plans, which we discussed in Chapter 5, in a sometimes shortsighted effort to reduce taxes *now*. They get a tax deferment this year, but it may not help at all in years to come.

Tax deferment in pretax plans may be nothing more than seeking instant grat-ification at a greater cost long term. In that sense it's not a lot different from spending your money on something you want, instead of investing it with the intention of getting a bigger reward at a later time. Just because you can reduce your taxes this year, don't think that you're avoiding them. You may not be. Plan for the longer term. Assess the tax consequences of your plan several years out or into retirement. That's what real planning does: it examines all the variables of your finances well into the future. Professional financial planners should be better at that than you are.

■ THE ONE QUESTION I'M ASKED MOST OFTEN

In my office, on the street, at parties, and on my radio show, I'm asked one question more than any other: *How do I determine the best way to take distributions from my retirement plan?*

The frequency with which I'm asked this question in the many forms it takes underscores the need to work with a professional planner. If you think the purpose of financial planning is only to accumulate assets, you aren't seeing half the picture.

With many more people retiring younger, in many cases still in their 50s, those people are spending as many years of their lives distributing assets as they spend accumulating them. Effective financial planning places equal importance on the second half of your life—the years when you are reaping the benefits of the first half or two-thirds of your life, your working years. Good financial planning not only helps you accumulate assets efficiently, but also helps you distribute them efficiently.

Many of my radio listeners and my clients are just beginning to think about distributions in their 50s, a time when it is already too late to avail themselves of some of the most effective accumulation and distribution strategies. If you're in your 50s or 60s, you can still make smart decisions to enhance your life and your wealth, but if you're in your 20s or 30s, you have so many more investment tools and vehicles to use. I think financial planners serve a very useful purpose if they do nothing more than get younger people to begin considering options and strategies. Begin planning your distribution strategy as you are planning your accumulation strategy.

As I wrote at the beginning of this book, the goal of enhancing your wealth is to enhance your life—however you choose to do it. A whole-life planning approach, a plan for your accumulation years as well as your distribution years, will help you do that. That's why you need the services of a good financial planner.

And by the way, I can't answer the question on distributions very effectively unless I know your full financial profile and your goals in life. That's because, like most people, you are not "average"—and taking advice aimed at "average" investors can be risky, as I have tried to point out.

■ 10 QUESTIONS YOU COULD ASK FINANCIAL PLANNERS: NINE GOOD, ONE WORTHLESS

OK. I hope that I've convinced you that using a financial planner is a good idea. Now, how do you go about choosing one that will deliver the value that justifies the cost? A good way to start is with a personal referral from someone whose opinion you value. However, even with a personal referral you should still interview the candidate yourself. Ultimately, I think the decision will be instinctive rather than intellectual.

Over the years, I've been interviewed by hundreds of people looking for someone to help them manage their finances. In the course of those interviews, I've learned what is useful to them—and I've developed a keen sense of what questions elicit information that I'd want if I were in their shoes. I've boiled it down to 10 questions. The first nine are useful, but the last, which is frequently asked, reveals nothing that will help you.

1. *What professional designations does the planner have?* The designation or lack of a designation does not necessarily indicate the competence of the planner. On the one hand, some people in the financial industry try to present themselves as financial planners in an attempt to enhance their credibility, even though they are

not qualified. On the other hand, pursuit of a professional designation can demonstrate a commitment to the financial planning profession. The designations that I deem relevant are:

- Certified Financial Planner (CFP)
- Chartered Financial Analyst (CFA)
- Chartered Financial Consultant (ChFC)
- Certified Public Accountant (CPA)
- Registered Financial Consultant (RFC)

2. *How many years has the planner been working in the industry and how did he or she get started?* There is a high attrition rate in the financial service industry. Many firms actually recruit representatives with the idea that the newly hired representative will establish accounts with friends and family and then ultimately fail and leave the industry, but the new clients will stay because they don't know where else to go.

3. *Has the planner ever been fined or suspended by a regulatory agency?* Consumer complaints are to be expected with a planner who's practiced a long time with a lot of clients. But to be fined or suspended indicates wrongdoing. There may be a reasonable explanation. Find out.

4. *How does he or she get paid?* Financial planners earn their compensation in four ways:
   - Fee for time
   - Fee for plan preparation
   - Commissions
   - Money management fees

The advantage of working with a "fee-only" planner, someone who charges a flat fee or hourly fee, is to avoid any conflict of interest because he or she is not trying to "sell" you anything. However, because the fee is the sole profit center, a fee-only planner is likely to charge significantly higher fees for his or her services. Therefore, many consumers who need financial help may find the cost of a fee-only planner prohibitive. Also, the single greatest reason a financial plan may fail to meet its objectives is that the client fails to implement the plan. (We all procrastinate to some degree.) A fee-only planner has no motivation to inspire clients to implement a plan, so it will be more likely to collect dust and become worthless.

It is also widely believed that if a planner receives commissions it will cost the investor more. That simply is not true. When you plan a vacation, do you call all the hotels in and around your ultimate destination? Do you personally check out all the times and costs of flights and then book your flight? How do you arrange your car rental? Many people make one call to a travel agent who will do all of those things for them. Furthermore, the cost is the same as (or even less than) if they arranged the trip themselves. Acquiring financial products is similar to planning a vacation with a travel agent. You can acquire products directly from the entity distributing the product or through an agent—the financial planner—and the fees and costs are often the same.

5. *Is the planner captive to a larger corporation? (Does he or she sell proprietary products?)* Many so-called financial planners are really product salespeople. If they are captive to a specific company, they may have a vested interest in selling that company's products. If I were a consumer shopping for a financial planner, I would want one who is independent—with a fiduciary responsibility to me and not to a parent company.

6. *How many clients does the planner have?* If the planner has very few clients, you might wonder how proficient he or she is. If he or she has too many clients, you may wonder about the level of service you will receive. Find out what you can expect from your planner. Then you will be able to measure whether or not he or she delivers.

7. *How many people does the planner have to support him or her? And what is their expertise?* Ask a prospective planner how big his or her staff is today and how big it was last year and the year before. It's important to know whether the organization is growing and the ratio of support staff to planners. The number of people in

support roles will tell you something about the level of service you will receive. To give you a benchmark for evaluating staff support, my firm has six staff people for every financial planner. I believe that's one of the best support ratios in our business.

8. *How does the planner address issues on which he or she is not an expert?* As I freely admit, I don't know all there is to know about financial planning. But I have formal working relationships with people whose job it is to follow and track developments in specific fields, such as taxes and accounting. In my company, we have hired those experts for our staff and they review every plan we put together. Their advice is invaluable to me—and I wouldn't be able to deliver the value I do to my clients without them. If the planners you interview do not have formal working relationships with such experts, find out how those issues will be resolved—and what it will cost you if outside assistance is required.

9. *What is the average net worth of the planner's clients or the range of clients he or she serves?* Financial planners may have a specialty or a focus that may not suit you. A financial planner who serves primarily clients who have net worths in the millions of dollars may not have the knowledge or

the interest in working with those who have less money to invest. You may get lost in the shuffle of big buck deals. On the other hand, if planners work primarily with people who have less money to invest, they may not know the intricacies of more advanced planning and investing techniques such as trusts and tax-advantaged investments. Such a planner may suit your needs now, but will he or she still be able to help you as your net worth grows?

Most of all, look for someone who listens to and understands what *you* want to accomplish. Less effective financial planners are as likely to fall victim to myths and to old habits as the average consumer. In the day-to-day crush of work, they may rely on off-the-shelf, one-size-fits-all investment strategies that are little better than the myths embraced by your Uncle Wilbur.

10. *Will the planner provide references?* Of course. Every planner will probably be able to provide names of clients who would give him or her a favorable recommendation. That's why I think asking for references is a waste of time. Don't bother. The planner will give you the names of only those who have a good opinion of the services they receive—and you don't know whether those people are astute investors. Are they qualified to evaluate the services they receive? You can only guess.

■ PREPARING TO MEET YOUR PLANNER—OR, CREATING YOUR OWN FINANCIAL PLAN, IF YOU INSIST

Choosing a financial planner isn't the end of your responsibility. Regardless of whom you choose, you are still the CEO of your money and it's up to you to ensure that you are gaining full value from your planner's services. No good planner can tell you what to do; a planner can only make recommendations. So you still need to supervise your planner and your plan. On the next few pages, I provide a framework for your decision-making.

Also, in recognition that some of you will still insist on giving a financial plan a try by yourself, the advice here will help you do it as well as possible—assuming that you enjoy all the disciplines involved in creating and implementing a good financial plan.

If you intend to create your own plan, however, you have to be brutally honest with yourself from the beginning. Many people have the best intentions when they sit down to create a plan and they might even do a pretty good job. But that's not where the biggest problems arise.

The real problems arise in the continuous management of that plan:

- preventing style drift in your portfolio or the funds in which you've invested;

- rebalancing regularly to maintain the ideal asset allocation;

- changing your allocation as your needs change;
- keeping abreast of tax changes that could give you a window of opportunity to alter your plan to your advantage.

After a while, many investors begin to let their plans slide; they get careless. Their portfolio no longer represents the asset allocation they selected. Or worse, their asset allocation reflects accurately their situation or needs of 10 years ago, even though their lives have changed dramatically. So think hard, not just about the knowledge you'll need to acquire or the time it will take to create a plan, but also about the commitment of time and energy to manage it effectively.

■ DREAM A LITTLE DREAM: KNOW WHERE YOU WANT TO GO

Slow down. Before you even begin to gather all the information you'll need to create an investment strategy, sit down on the porch or patio or in front of the fireplace (with your spouse or partner, if any) and let your mind roam.

What do you really want from life? If you could do anything you want, what would you do? Don't put financial restrictions on yourself now. Dream. Stretch a little. Once you have that dream defined, once you know roughly where you want to go, you can begin to determine what role a financial plan can play in helping you live that dream.

■ GATHER ALL YOUR FINANCIAL INFORMATION: KNOW WHERE YOU ARE

The second step is to gather all the information you will need. You can't plan unless you know where you are. In my practice, I ask my clients to obtain the documents and provide the information noted below.

■ DOCUMENTS

Get together the following financial and legal documents:

- Federal and state income tax returns for at least two years
- Most recent pay stubs
- Statements from all investment accounts
- Documentation of all company retirement, investment, and insurance plans, including benefits and costs
- All personal life, health, disability, long-term care, and Medicare supplement policies and statements
- Estate planning documents such as wills, trusts, powers of attorney, and living wills (if you don't have a will, this is an excellent time to prepare one)
- Documentation related to involvement in all business or personal matters that could affect your personal financial situation, such as buy/sell agreements, non-compete agreements, consulting

agreements, and deferred compensation plans

- Social Security and pension benefit estimates

■ ASSETS AND LIABILITIES

Make a list of all of your assets and liabilities—and, if you are planning with a spouse, be sure to note which assets are in whose name or if they are jointly held.

When you list your liabilities, be sure to include complete information on your loans for your primary residence, second home, cars, boats, and other recreational vehicles. This information should include original balance, current balance, monthly payment, length of loan, and the interest rate, as well as whether those obligations are personal or jointly held.

For any fixed-interest investments, list the current value and the interest rate. For equity investments, list the average growth rate for each stock or mutual fund. List your taxable, tax-deferred, and tax-free investments separately. Be sure to include any insurance policies, including disability insurance, company-sponsored plans, and annuities.

For each asset that you own, also include the amount you add to that investment each month or each year.

■ INCOME AND EXPENSES

You're not finished identifying where you are yet, because you still have to determine all of your income and expenses.

Don't calculate only your present income; try to project expected annual increases as a percentage of your present income. You want to have as clear a picture of your future income as possible. Include wages and salary, bonuses, self-employment income, interests or dividends on investments, Social Security, rental property income, pensions, alimony, and any loans you've made.

Make a realistic effort to determine what your living expenses are for a year. It may be easiest to break it down monthly and then add those up to get your yearly expenses. This is a good exercise in financial discipline by itself, because most people don't think they're spending as much as they are. When determining your expenses, be sure to add any estimated major expenses you will incur in the future, such as college education costs for your children.

■ THE IMMEDIATE FIRST STEPS TO A BETTER FINANCIAL FUTURE

If you're like a lot of Americans, by the time you finish determining where you are, you'll already see one or two things that you will have to do immediately to align your finances with your dream:

1. You'll have consumer debt you have to pay off. That's the top priority. Make a plan to pay off that debt now. Very few investments can consistently earn a return high enough to justify carrying consumer debt at 15% to 21%. Once you pay that off, you'll have

another $50, $100, $200, or more a month that you're now paying in interest to invest—without changing your lifestyle at all.

2. You'll see that your expenses are eating up more than 90% of your after-tax income. The first step is to reduce your expenses so that you can save or invest 10% of your income. This is really where you will decide if your dream means anything to you. If you aren't willing to cut back a bit each month on what you spend— and most of that overspending is probably on impulse purchases that have no significant impact on your happiness—then your dream isn't very compelling.

■ PLOT A COURSE TO REACH YOUR DREAM DESTINATION

Without knowing your specific financial situation, it would be irresponsible of me to provide more detailed advice on how to create your plan. If you learn one thing from this book, I hope it is that no solution fits everyone and every circumstance. Your individual plan must fit your unique life and dream. That's precisely why many of the myths I've attacked here are myths: they probably don't apply to your situation.

I can, however, suggest a few important things for you to consider in your plan, whether you are working alone or with a financial planner. Determine the following:

1. Your asset allocation

2. The tax consequences of investments, income, and distributions

3. The efficiency of your money.

• *Asset Allocation*

If you have money invested already, the next step is to look at your asset allocation. Do you have a mix of asset classes that will help you achieve your goals? Is all your money invested in one or two asset classes? Are they aggressive enough or conservative enough that you can reach your goals without pulling out all your hair because they are riskier than you can tolerate?

• *Tax Consequences*

You'll also be able to see at a glance if you are using all three tax file cabinets that we discussed in Chapter 2. Are all of your assets in one tax file cabinet? Do you have a lot of tax-deferred investments, but no taxable or tax-advantaged assets?

The goal is to reduce your taxes as much as possible, but be sure to look at tax liability from two perspectives. The first is liability on the accumulation of your assets. The second is liability on the distribution of your assets.

Most people do a very good job of reducing taxes during accumulation, primarily by making significant contributions to pretax retirement plans. Most people do not do as well, however, at reducing taxes on distributions. Have you done any tax planning for your retirement? Millions of people take action to reduce a comparatively small tax per year while they're working. But in retirement, after they've accumulated a significant amount of money, they do nothing to plan for tax reduction when they need it most. Reducing taxes on the accumulation of the money is less significant if you don't also reduce taxes on the distribution.

A quick review of asset allocation and tax consequences leads you naturally to the third key in determining a basic direction for your future: investment efficiency.

- *Investment Efficiency*

Investment efficiency is again a determination that must be made in each individual case. Some things are obvious: for instance, leaving money to accumulate in a taxable fixed-interest account is almost never efficient, because you are compounding your tax liability. But so many of the variables that will determine the efficiency of your investments will depend on your personality and your circumstances. I have addressed briefly below a few of the most critical variables that you should consider as you begin to formulate your plan.

1. Competitive Returns. Competitive returns obviously will mean different things to different people. A 65-year-old whose primary objective is income or estate preservation might be happy with 5%. But, a 30-year-old invested in small cap stocks is likely expecting far more than that. The key here is to perform equal to or better than the average in the asset class in which you're investing. In other words, comparing a CD with a mutual fund is unfair. Comparing a large-cap fund with a small-cap fund is also unrealistic. However, comparing large cap with large cap is appropriate.

Remember also that in any given year about 75% of mutual funds underperform the S&P 500 index. If you use mutual funds, find those that beat the index consistently. Even better, in my opinion, use actively managed, broadly diversified institutional equity funds. Unfortunately these can be accessed in most cases only through investment professionals, so they are not available to you if you do your own investing. That's one reason why, even if you're capable of creating and managing your own plan, you may want to consider working with a financial planner who has access to this type of fund.

A rule of thumb that may be useful to you in calculating the rate of return that you will need to achieve your goals is the Rule of 72, which is widely used in the investment community. Using this rule, you divide the percentage rate of return on an investment into the number 72 to determine how long it will take to double your money. For example, a 6% return will double your money in 12 years. (72 /6 = 12.)

Years to Double Your Money

Rate of Return*	Years to Double
6%	12.0
8%	9.0
10%	7.2
12%	6.0

* The rate of return is for illustration only and does not represent any specific investment. A note about the Rule of 72: securities tend to fluctuate in value and return on a daily basis so it is impossible to tell with any certainty how long it will take to double in value.

Figure 8.1

2. Risk. When most people think of risk, they think of whether they can afford to lose money. Many of those people decide not to risk losing any money, so they put it into fixed-interest investments— where inflation and taxes will almost certainly negate their interest earnings and perhaps even erode the purchasing power of their principal. I think that's an enormous risk. It's way too risky for me.

People commonly believe that to increase rates of return it's necessary to also increase risk—and that's true of investing in any single asset class. But we have many asset classes to choose from and many of them have some degree of negative correlation. We can balance our risk, not eliminate it, by diversifying assets among various classes. Investors with a greater risk tolerance can choose an asset balance tilted more heavily toward volatile, higher-risk equities. More conservative investors can choose an asset balance that gives a heavier weight to less volatile investments—but still have some money invested in higher-risk asset classes.

Don't look at risk in terms of the two extremes—either losing all your money or earning practically nothing on all your money. Think instead in terms of what percentage of your money you want to keep perfectly safe and what percentage of your money you're willing to risk in exchange for the potential for higher returns that historically have been available.

Especially if your investment in higher-risk equities is in mutual funds, it's unlikely that you will lose all or even most of your money. Mutual fund managers aren't likely to stand by and watch while stocks that they own fall to zero. And even if they were willing to do that, they've balanced their portfolios with other stocks that are intended to provide different returns.

In this day of highly priced stocks and phenomenal returns, perhaps you're in greater danger of making too many highly speculative investments than making choices that are too conservative. For those of you addicted to .com and Internet stocks, I'd recommend investing some money in boring REITs, which have the potential to provide a fairly certain though conservative return. Believe it or not, what REITs are returning as of this writing was considered a pretty good return on investment once—and may well be again some day, probably sooner rather than later.

3. Systematic Investment. A successful financial plan is consistently nourished. You don't just put money in once and then sit back and watch it grow. You must constantly add money. Ideally, everyone should invest at least 10% of his or her income. If you can't live on 90% of what you're making, you're living beyond your means and should alter your lifestyle.

The discipline of regular investing also will encourage you to reexamine regularly your asset allocation and to rebalance your portfolio. If you make regular additions to your investment accounts, you can put that new money into the asset class or classes that will keep your portfolio balanced.

4. Liquidity, Availability, and Flexibility. Too many people are tying up too much of their money in pretax plans. Americans frequently finance purchases of cars, furniture, home improvements, landscaping, VCRs, computers, and other products because they have no accessible cash. But they have a lot of money in pretax plans that

they cannot access. When you subtract a lifetime of interest costs on consumer loans from the internal earnings of the pretax plan, the net return of the pretax plan is greatly reduced.

Of course, the need to have access to savings or investments will vary greatly among individuals. In general, tax-advantaged and tax-deferred investments require a longer time commitment and the money is less likely to be available on short notice than with most taxable investments. That's one of the important reasons that you shouldn't ignore the first tax file cabinet either, taxable investments.

Taking distributions out of your financial plan should be easy. (That doesn't mean, however, that you should consider only investment vehicles that are relatively liquid, such as widely traded equities or mutual funds.) Also consider what procedures you must follow to liquidate or redeem any investments. If you don't know, ask!

Frequently we're forced to wait weeks or complete a mountain of paperwork just to receive some of *our own* money! There's no reason it should be difficult to get your hands on your money. Also be aware of any redemption penalties that may be applied to your investments. If you redeem a CD before its expiration, for instance, you may have to pay a penalty. Some mutual funds also impose redemption fees, if you want to redeem your shares before a specified length of time. You'll avoid a lot of confusion and aggravation if you know before you invest what you must do to get your money back and any price you have to pay to do so.

5. *The Worst Case.* The ideal plan has contingencies for complications that may occur. What if the primary wage earner loses his or her job? What if someone dies suddenly? What if you become disabled? Ask yourself whether your financial plan will still succeed if an unforeseen emergency strikes your family. Will you still be able to save and invest and have a secure financial future?

Many of the financial plans that I review, whether done by another professional or by an individual, will break down and fail under the worst of circumstances. A plan may look great if life stays rosy, but, unfortunately, life is not always rosy. The ideal plan succeeds in best and worst cases.

An important component of worst-case planning is *property and casualty insurance*. Property and casualty insurance generally refers to auto and homeowner's insurance. Most Americans have deductibles that are too low and do not carry enough liability protection.

The lower the deductible, the higher the premium. Let's assume that our auto insurance has a deductible of $250. If we raise the deductible to $500, it saves $50 in premium. If we go only five years without a claim, we can self-insure and be ahead. Even in a worst case scenario of having an accident and filing a claim every year, it still costs only an extra $250 per year, which has a minimal financial impact on us.

Deductibles should always be at least $500, if not $1,000.

Consider the following scenario. Your husband is 35, earns $50,000 per year, and plans to work at least 20 more years. That means he would earn $1,000,000 in those 20 years. But your husband dies in an auto accident caused by a drunk driver who has only $100,000 of liability coverage on his auto policy—not atypical for Americans. That person's insurance carrier sends you a check for $100,000. How do you feel? What would you do? Would you consult an attorney and file a lawsuit against the drunken driver? Of course you would, because $100,000 is only a small fraction of the economic value of your deceased spouse.

Now, reverse the situation. What if you make a driving error and someone is seriously hurt or killed. Do you think you are likely to be sued? Of course you are! To protect yourself from this potential financial devastation costs roughly the same as carrying the lower deductibles you had. The liability limits should be increased on auto/homeowner's and an umbrella or personal liability policy should be placed over that. Liability coverage is one of the most important, necessary, and affordable things you can ever buy. No matter how much money you make, how much net worth you have, or how great a return you get from your investment portfolio, without proper liability protection you are only a slip on a banana peel away from financial devastation.

Life changes quickly. Many people

commit to investment strategies that they cannot reverse when their life situation changes. It's virtually impossible to anticipate all of our future needs today. Advances in technology, tax law changes, planned obsolescence, and a propensity to consume will complicate and cause changes in our lives. We must have a plan that is adaptable.

■ THE NEXT STEP: INVESTING!

After you've determined asset allocation and tax consequences and considered each of the variables in investment efficiency, then it's time—and only then—to select your specific investment vehicles. You'll find advice and opinions on specific investments almost without trying. There's no shortage of magazines, books, TV shows, and Web sites touting or analyzing investments. With such a wealth of information, you should never have to rely on just one source for information. Seek information from multiple sources before you invest.

■ CONCLUSION

A financial planner should be able to provide value that justifies the cost of his or her services—and should be willing to explain that value. The reasons for choosing someone to help formulate and execute a financial plan to achieve a dream will vary from one person to another as much as the dreams themselves. Whether you lack the time, the expertise, or the stomach for worry to create your own financial plan, a

professional should be able to provide valuable assistance.

The financial authors and magazines that are critical of various planning and investment strategies due to cost, frequently overlook the benefits that are purchased by that cost. In hiring a financial planner, as in determining the execution of your investment strategy, focus on value instead of just cost.

Choosing a financial planner is intensely personal. You will reveal information to your planner that you would reveal to very few others—and you will give that planner an extraordinary responsibility for helping you achieve your dream. Beyond the empirical or factual evidence of a financial planner's ability to meet your needs, you have to trust that person and place your confidence in him or her. All facts being equal, trust your intuition. If you actually like that person and enjoy your interaction with him or her, the process of achieving your dream will be much more enjoyable—and never forget that enjoying life is the ultimate purpose of money.

Whether you use a financial planner or create your own plan without expert assistance, always remember that you are in control of your money. Someone else may sweat the details, someone else may take the worry of day-to-day money management off your shoulders, but you are the CEO of your money. When you hear or read advice from any source about how to create wealth, think carefully about what you're hearing or reading and whether it applies to you and your situation. A lot of conventional wisdom doesn't apply to you, whether you hear it from your friends, your relatives, or your financial adviser.

■ HELMER'S HINTS

- Do you enjoy reading the case studies in this book, doing the calculations to double-check my numbers, or considering alternatives to my suggestions? If you don't, financial planners exist for your benefit. Hire one. If you do enjoy all the details and have an aptitude for this stuff, you might be one of those (very few in my experience) who are capable of doing most of the work of financial planning and investing yourself.

- Trust your gut. Working to achieve your dream should be fun. Your comfort level with your financial adviser is an important factor.

- Always interview any financial planner in person before you agree to do business with him or her.

- Ask questions. If you're reluctant to ask questions for fear of appearing naive or uninformed, you're working with the wrong financial planner. It's your money. No question is stupid; no financial planner is very good if he or she makes you think a question is stupid.

- When you sit down to create a financial plan, begin with your dreams.

- Allocate assets carefully among different asset classes in a way that optimizes potential return for the level of risk you're comfortable with.

- Take into account the tax consequences of every investment and reduce taxes whenever you can. You probably need to consult a tax professional to determine what your options may be. Your plan should consider taxes on distributions of earnings as well as on the accumulation of money invested.

- Don't look at risk as all or nothing; it's rarely like that in the investment world. Higher risk may pose little threat if balanced properly, while lower risk may pose a greater threat if not balanced properly.

- Don't take shortcuts. Use a systematic approach to determine your goals, identify your resources, allocate your assets, and choose your investments.

- And don't even bother to begin creating a financial plan if you aren't committed to staying on top of it, reevaluating it, rebalancing it, and reassessing the tax consequences regularly.

GIVING STRATEGIES: DO GOOD, FEEL GOOD, AND LIVE WELL

The Myth: Giving money to charities is only for those who want to do good or feel good.

The Reality: Charitable giving strategies offer significant economic benefits for the giver.

For so many people in these affluent times, giving money to a church, a charity, a community or arts organization, or an educational institution is a primary motivation for financial planning. Even for many of my clients who don't have large net worths, giving some money to others is very important either during their lives or upon their deaths.

I believe strongly in the importance of making charitable donations, and I've been pleased to be able to work with many clients who have made very generous contributions to their favorite non-profit organizations. They have been delighted to make those gifts— and to discover that they received very significant economic benefits from their generosity.

I've written this brief chapter to introduce some of the basic concepts of charitable giving, so that you can be better informed as you discuss the possibilities with your financial planner,

your attorney, or the organization to which you wish to contribute. Giving can be a rewarding part of your investment strategy and you can do it in ways that benefit yourself as well as your favorite organizations or causes.

■ DON'T TRY THIS AT HOME

These giving strategies are not do-it-yourself undertakings. You will need assistance from professionals to do it properly, so that you and the organization to which you are contributing obtain the maximum benefit from your gift.

Many charitable, religious, and educational organizations will provide considerable assistance to you in handling the legal and accounting aspects of making a gift to them. It makes sense to discuss your desires and plans with the organization as early as possible to make the most of its assistance and expertise.

What those organizations may not be able to provide, however, is advice on where your gift fits in your overall plan. Will your gift create unanticipated hardship for you at some point? Is your gift actually much smaller than you would like to give and could comfortably afford to give if your money were working more efficiently? These questions can be answered only in the context of a complete financial plan that takes into account your needs and your investment strategy.

■ WHY WOULD YOU DO IT?

I've encountered nearly every reason imaginable for making contributions to charitable organizations. The most common, however, are:

1. Compassion for those in need
2. Religious and spiritual commitment
3. Desire to perpetuate one's beliefs, values, and ideals
4. Support for the arts, sciences, and education
5. A desire to share "good fortune" with others

The tax laws of the United States encourage these gifts by granting tax deductions for them in many cases. The reasoning is the same as when the IRS allows deductions for investments in energy and affordable housing: if individual citizens help meet our country's needs voluntarily, it reduces the responsibility of the government. Many would also argue that private support of charitable activities is more efficient than public support.

But because of the tax treatment of charitable contributions, individuals may realize not only immediate tax benefits, but also advantages in terms of after-tax cash flow and the size of the estate they may pass on to their heirs. Gifts to charity during lifetime or at death, if structured properly, will reduce

the size of the taxable estate. An additional benefit of lifetime gifts is that an income tax deduction is available within certain percentage limitations.

How can giving money away provide economic benefits beyond the tax deduction? Let's consider the case of Howard and Betty.

They were in their early 60s when they came to me. They had owned and operated a family farm for 40 years, but they were preparing to sell their farm for $1.2 million to a real estate developer. Their cost in the property, or basis, was about $200,000, so they would have a gain of $1 million. That gain would be taxed as a long-term capital gain at a federal rate of 20%, for a liability of $200,000. This was a big tax liability, but they would still net $1 million after taxes. Assuming a fairly conservative hypothetical investment rate of return of 8% on a portfolio, the proceeds from the farm sale would generate $80,000 income per year without invading the principal.

During an introductory meeting with Howard and Betty, I discovered two very important things. First, they were very spiritual people who gave a lot to their church and wanted to do even more. Second, even though they felt blessed to have an $800,000 gain on their land, they were unhappy about having to pay $200,000 in taxes, but they felt there was nothing they could do about it.

I advised Howard and Betty to create a charitable remainder trust (CRT) and fund the trust with the property. Then the CRT would sell the land to the developer. Because the asset would be sold through the CRT, there would be no capital gains tax liability for Howard and Betty. The CRT would provide them with an income stream of $96,000 per year (8% x $1.2 million) instead of $80,000. They would also receive a tax deduction now for the future gift to their church, because when they passed away, the balance of the trust (the remainder) would go to the church. The gift they could make to their church was the primary motivating factor for Howard and Betty to pursue this strategy, but it also gave them an extra $16,000 of income each year that they could have obtained no other way.

The one flaw that Betty and Howard saw in the plan was that they would be disinheriting their children. Although they wanted to give a lot to their church, they didn't want to leave nothing for their children. We solved the problem by using the tax deduction over five years and fully paying for a $1 million last survivor or second-to-die life insurance policy, so their children would have $1 million tax-free to split after Betty and Howard passed away. This strategy would allow Howard and Betty not only to provide for their children, but also to increase the money their children would divide by $400,000, because the $1 million life insurance benefit would not be calculated as part of their taxable estate.

The result of this strategy was to:

- Make a profound gift to their church

- Increase Howard and Betty's annual income

- Generate a significant tax deduction they could spread over five years

- Protect their children's inheritance by using the tax savings created by the deduction to purchase life insurance with essentially no out-of-pocket cost.

Howard and Betty felt very good about their gift, which certainly did a lot of good for their church, and they also increased their income and the money they left to their children.

■ GIVING SOONER OR LATER: DIFFERENT TYPES OF CHARITABLE GIFTS

Tax laws pertaining to charitable contributions can be very complex—and allow for many types of gifts.

Gifts. The simplest form of donation in terms of tax treatment is an outright gift of cash or other valuable assets. Within certain limitations, such gifts generate income tax deductions at the time the gift is made—and reduce the size of the taxable estate.

Wills. Individuals who might depend on income from their assets to meet their needs often designate a portion of their estate to go to a charity upon their death. Such a bequest, if properly structured, will reduce the size of a taxable estate.

Split-Interest Gifts. A method of charitable giving that is widely used is much more complicated—and can take many forms. In the interest of simplicity, I will provide a very general description of this type of gift. Please consult professionals to determine the various forms these gifts may take.

A split-interest gift operates on the principle that any sum of money or valuable property is valued in two ways—as the value of the thing itself, or the principal, and as the value of the income stream or earning power of that asset. For instance, if you have $10,000, you have not only the money but also the potential to earn a return on that money. With a split-interest gift, you either donate the principal, but retain the income stream from that gift for your life, or donate the earning power of that asset, which reverts to your estate upon your death.

Most plans under which you make a gift but retain the income from that gift are called charitable *remainder* trusts. You receive income from that gift, but the remainder, the underlying asset, goes to the charitable organization when you die or after a predetermined period of time. One of the tax advantages of this type of gift is that, in many cases, the tax deduction for the remainder gift may be taken when the gift is made.

Remainder trusts are especially attractive when donating highly appreciated assets, such as stocks that have been owned for a long period of time. In most cases, the donor does not have to pay capital gains taxes on the appreciation of that asset, yet can take a tax deduction, within IRS limitations, for that gift.

The other type of split-interest gift is usually called a charitable *lead* trust. In that case, you donate income earned by an asset, but the asset reverts to your estate upon your death.

You may have heard the names of many well-used vehicles for making split-interest gifts to charitable, religious, and educational organizations:

- charitable remainder annuity trust (CRAT)
- charitable remainder unitrust (CRUT)
- pooled income fund (PIF)
- charitable gift annuity
- charitable lead annuity trust (CLAT)
- charitable lead unitrust (CLUT)

In case you're wondering (and most people do), the primary difference between an annuity trust and a unitrust is in the form of income paid by the asset: an annuity trust pays out a fixed dollar amount while a unitrust pays out a fixed percentage.

Your individual situation will determine which of these methods will be most advantageous for you and the organization to which you are making a donation. Each of them generates different income tax and estate tax consequences. Each of them may also have different gift tax consequences, if you designate others, such as your children or grandchildren, as the beneficiaries of your interest in the trust.

■ CONCLUSION

Tax laws have created several ways to make tax-advantaged donations to charitable, religious, and educational organizations—almost all of them complex and all worth considering if you wish to donate a portion of your wealth. You may find that a gift to your favorite charity, if structured properly, may actually increase your after-tax cash flow during your lifetime. Moreover, your charitable contributions enable you to decide how your money is used, rather than letting the government decide.

It may seem to be a lot of hassle to go through just to give your money away—but it would be inefficient for you and your favorite charity to *not* take advantage of the tax breaks available by doing it the IRS way.

■ HELMER'S HINTS

- Your charitable gift may provide economic benefits to you and your heirs. While that may not be your primary motivation for giving, it can be a very attractive fringe benefit—one that is readily available and could be used by many more people if they planned carefully.

- Get professional help. The last thing you want is for neither you nor your heirs nor your favorite charitable organization to receive the benefit of your generosity. The IRS has very strict rules on what is permissible if you are doing anything more complicated than making a straight cash gift.

EASY REFERENCE GUIDE TO INVESTMENTS AND WEALTH ENHANCEMENT

I may have made reference at some point in this book to an investment vehicle that you didn't understand. My apologies. In order to help you gain a better understanding of investments you don't know well, but without interrupting my outrage at the myths I've been attacking, I've included in this quick reference guide a brief description of many investment options.

While these descriptions are accurate, they do not go into the detail that you may require. If you want more detail, it may mean you have a great enough interest in and aptitude for finances and investing that you will easily find additional sources of information. There are entire books about many of the investments I cover briefly. While I have not covered every nuance or variable in these investing options, I have provided my opinions of their general utility and efficiency in most financial plans. I have grouped these investment options in five broad categories:

- fixed-interest investments
- equities
- annuities
- pretax retirement plans (including new IRAs)
- life insurance

■ FIXED-INTEREST INVESTMENTS

STATEMENT SAVINGS ACCOUNTS

"Statement savings account" is the name for what was once known as a "passbook" savings account. Statement savings accounts usually accept small deposits with no minimum balance, have no fixed maturity date, and earn relatively low interest rates. They are savings accounts only in the sense that you are not spending the money. But if it's money you don't intend to spend or need to keep in reserve for a short-term emergency, it doesn't belong here. It's not an investment.

Advantages: Liquid. Fixed rate of interest. FDIC-insured. Good for emergency reserves or short-term savings.

Disadvantages: Low yield. Taxes and inflation can exceed the interest gains, so that the account actually loses purchasing power over time.

MONEY MARKET ACCOUNTS

Money market accounts are a good place to put money temporarily until you are ready to invest in something more productive. You could think of them as the equivalent of a piggy bank. Money market accounts typically have some level of minimum balance requirement, are as safe as savings or checking accounts, but offer greater interest rates than statement savings accounts and more flexibility than certificates of deposit (CDs).

Advantages: Excellent intermediate-term savings for something such as a down payment for a home within a year or two or next year's college tuition.

Disadvantages: Poor long-term returns compared with the stock market.

CERTIFICATES OF DEPOSIT

Certificates of deposit (CDs) are one of the most conservative investments you can make. They are cash deposits that you promise to keep at a bank for a predetermined period of time, generally ranging from one or two months to as long as five years. In return for your promise to keep the money deposited at the bank for the predetermined time, the bank promises to return your "original principal" (the money deposited) *plus* a predetermined rate of interest. CDs, like other bank deposits, are federally insured up to a total of $100,000 and are very easy to buy—some banks even let you buy CDs over the telephone.

Advantages: Simple. Convenient. Safe.

Disadvantages: Illiquid. Should never be used in IRAs or other pretax plans.

UNITED STATES GOVERNMENT SECURITIES

U.S. government securities are "direct obligations" of the federal government and are backed by the "full faith and credit" of the government. In terms of default risk, these bonds are widely considered to be the safest debt investment available. Another feature of U.S. government bonds, typically considered beneficial to the bondholder, is that interest income is generally not taxed at either the state or the local level.

- *Savings Bonds.* The federal government started its savings bond program in 1935 to provide a refuge for individual savings that would be free from market fluctuation. Unlike "marketable" Treasury securities, savings bonds are not traded on any exchange. The U.S. government is both the issuer and ultimate purchaser of all savings bonds. Three types of savings bonds are currently available:

- **Series EE Bonds.** Series EE bonds can be purchased at banks and other financial institutions. A savings bond is purchased at 50% of its face value, in amounts ranging from $50 to $10,000. For example, the purchaser of a $50 savings bond will pay $25. Interest is "earned" by gradual increases in the value of the bond; interest is credited to the value of the bond every six months. Yields will vary, depending on market rates and the length of time the bond has been held. The bonds can be cashed any time after six months. Current EE bonds have a maturity of 17 years; however with extensions, the bonds can continue to earn interest for up to 30 years. Holders of EE bonds can choose to be taxed each year on the increase in value or to defer taxation until the bonds are cashed.

- **Series HH Bonds.** Unlike series EE bonds, HH bonds pay interest to the bondholder every six months. Yields are fixed, but can change after 10 years. The interest from HH bonds is taxable each year. These bonds are issued in four denominations—$500, $1,000, $5,000, and $10,000—and mature in 20 years. Series HH bonds cannot be purchased for cash; they can be acquired only at federal reserve banks in exchange for E/EE bonds or matured Series H bonds. (Series E bonds were issued from 1941 to 1980, series H bonds from 1952 to 1979.)

- **Series I Bonds.** I bonds are a new creation, inflation-indexed bonds backed by the U.S. government. The bonds earn interest through application of a composite rate: a fixed rate that remains the same for the life of the bond and an inflation rate based on the Consumer Price Index (CPI-U) that changes twice a year. I bonds may be purchased in denominations as low as $50, with a maximum purchase in any one year of $30,000. They will earn interest for up to 30 years, although they may be redeemed at any time after six months; however, I bonds held for less than five years incur an interest penalty. Interest accrues monthly and is compounded semiannually. Interest earnings are payable upon redemption of the bonds. The earnings are exempt from state and local income taxes.

- **"Marketable" U.S. Government Securities.** There are several types of "marketable" government debt securities; they receive their name because they are widely traded in public markets. Existing and new marketable U.S. government bonds can be purchased through government securities dealers, usually for a small commission. Alternatively, new issues may be purchased directly from the government without paying commission, through the Bureau of Public Debt's Treasury Direct program.

- **Treasury Bills.** Treasury bills, commonly called "T-bills," are short-term debt obligations, with maturities of 13, 26, or 52 weeks. They are sold at a discount from face value; the difference between the purchase price and the face value is the "interest." The interest is not taxable until the bill is sold or at maturity. The minimum initial investment is $10,000.

- **Treasury Notes.** Treasury notes, or T-notes, are medium-term debt obligations, with maturities ranging from one to 10 years. Notes have a fixed interest rate and pay interest semiannually. Notes with maturities of one to five years have a $5,000 minimum investment; longer-term treasury notes have a $1,000 minimum.

- **Treasury Bonds.** Treasury bonds, or T-bonds, have maturities greater than 10 years. Like T-notes, T-bonds have a fixed interest rate and pay interest semiannually.

- **Treasury Inflation-Protection Securities.** Treasury Inflation-Protection Securities (TIPS) are a new type of government debt. With a fixed percentage yield and interest paid every six months, TIPS are intended to provide protection against loss of purchasing power due to inflation. At issue, TIPS have a par value of the principal amount; the value of the principal amount is adjusted for changes up or down in the Consumer Price Index (CPI-U). Each interest payment is calculated by multiplying the adjusted principal amount by the fixed percentage rate. At maturity, the investor receives the greater of the inflation-adjusted principal amount or the face value at original issue.

- **Other Government Securities.** There are a number of debt securities available that are widely considered "government bonds." These debt instruments are normally issued under authority of an act of Congress and usually involve some form of government guarantee or sponsorship. Most are freely traded in public markets. These securities come in different forms and are issued by entities such as the Government National Mortgage Association (GNMA), the Federal National Mortgage Association (FNMA), or the Federal Financing Bank (FFB).

Not all of these securities are backed by the "full faith and credit" of the U.S. government. Furthermore, interest income from these securities may or may not be exempt from state and local income tax. Therefore, investors need to be aware of what the underlying securities for their bonds are and what tax liability the interest income carries.

Advantages: Extremely safe. Potential tax advantages.

Disadvantages: Low yields. Confusing. No service.

ZERO COUPON BONDS

The term "coupon" refers to a bond's interest rate. The name originated at a time when coupons were actually attached to bond certificates. Each coupon represented six months' worth of interest, so twice each year the bondholder would clip the coupon from the certificate and take it to the bank to redeem for cash. So the word "coupon" became synonymous with interest rate.

Is it true, then, that zero coupon bonds pay no interest? If so, why would anyone want to buy them? All bond certificates feature a face value that is the amount the issuer must pay when the bond matures. Therefore, the

bond's face value is not necessarily the same as its price. People are willing to buy zero coupon bonds (bonds with no interest) because they buy them for a price substantially below their face value. This is known as "buying at a discount." At maturity, the issuer pays you the full face value; the difference between the purchase price and the face value is equal to the interest the bond should have earned. Please note, however, that the "phantom" interest accruing is taxable.

Advantages: None.

Disadvantages: Paying taxes on phantom income that hasn't yet been received.

CORPORATE BONDS

A company wants to raise capital to purchase a new plant and equipment, for example, or to fund research and development for future growth. One way to do so is to encourage investors to lend money to the company in return for a promised interest rate and a return of their initial investment within a predetermined number of years. This is essentially the definition of a corporate bond. Stated another way, corporate bonds are debt instruments issued by large corporations.

Corporate bonds issued today are usually registered with the Securities and Exchange Commission (SEC) and pay interest semiannually. Maturities typically range from one to 30 years. By way of contrast, bonds issued in the 19th century were often bearer bonds with detachable coupons. The owner of a bond had to clip a coupon every six months and return it to the bond issuer for payment. Maturities could reach up to 100 years.

There are a number of types of corporate bonds:

- *Mortgage Bonds:* Bonds secured by identifiable assets, such as real estate or equipment.

- *Debentures:* Bonds secured only by the faith and credit of the issuer.

- *Convertible Bonds:* Bonds that can be converted into a specific number of shares of the common stock of the issuing corporation. An investor who buys a convertible bond usually expects the price of the underlying common stock to rise over time.

- *Commercial Paper:* Commercial paper is used to meet very short-term (30-90 days) corporate financing needs. It is essentially an unsecured "IOU."

Occasionally, corporate bonds will have additional features:

- *Sinking Fund:* Some bonds require the issuing corporation to make regular payments into a special, dedicated fund, designed to ensure that interest and principal payments are made when due.

- *Call Feature:* Bonds issued during periods of high interest rates may have a feature that allows the issuer to redeem or "call" the bond prior to maturity. If a bond is called, the issuer will normally redeem the bond for full face value or with a slight premium. Such bonds usually have an initial period of time during which the call feature cannot be used.

- *Put Feature:* If a bond has this feature, it allows the investor to force the corporation to redeem the bond and "put" the bond back where it came from, usually at face value.

Advantages: "Investment grade" bonds are generally safer than ownership of the company through stock. Slightly higher interest rates than government bonds backed by the U.S. government.

Disadvantages: Historically lower returns than ownership.

MUNICIPAL BONDS

State and local governments issue municipal bonds. They have been a primary source of capital for state and local governments for hundreds of years and are considered a very safe investment. There are two types of municipal bonds: general obligation (GO) and revenue.

GO bonds are guaranteed by the government issuing the bond. Revenue bonds are not guaranteed. GO bonds usually raise money for public works that do not generate revenue, such as highways. Revenue bonds are usually backed by the anticipated revenue from the project they are funding. A revenue bond could be used to fund a toll road, for example, but if the project fails to raise enough revenue, the bond could default. For this reason, GO bonds are considered safer than revenue bonds.

Municipal bonds are extremely popular. Most investors are attracted to municipal bonds because the interest on them is generally free of federal income taxes. Many states also exempt investors from taxes if the bond is issued by the state in which the investor lives.

Most municipal bonds are callable, which means that the municipality that issued your bond can at its discretion redeem the bond before it matures. In other words, it can give you your money back early. Assume, for example, that your local government issues a bond at a hypothetical 8% and interest rates in general subsequently drop to 4%. The government would save a lot of money if it could cancel all of those 8% bonds, return the principal to the investors, then issue fresh bonds at the new current rate of 4%. In other words, if you buy a long-term bond expecting a high interest rate for many years, you could find yourself getting all of your money back much sooner. You would likely be forced to reinvest at a lower rate. As a taxpayer, you would be happy to see your local government save money by refinancing its debt at lower rates, but as an investor you would be

disappointed. However, if interest rates rise from 8% to 10%, the government would not call the bonds. The government will call bonds only when there's a financial advantage in doing so.

Advantages: Generally safe, potentially tax-free. An excellent equity hedge for investors in high tax brackets, because the higher the percentage of your income you have to pay in taxes, the greater the value of bonds' tax-free status.

Disadvantages: Generally lower yields than "investment grade" corporate bonds. (Bond issuers that can't offer tax-free status have to pay higher interest rates to attract lenders.) A terrible investment for investors in a low tax bracket.

■ EQUITIES

STOCKS

In the previous section I described how a company can sell corporate bonds to raise needed capital. The second way in which a company can raise capital is by selling part of the company; in other words, it can issue stock. The investors who purchase part of the company are called stockholders. These investors have no way of determining their rate of return. If the value of the company significantly increases, the price per share of the stock will rise accordingly and the stockholder will have a very attractive rate of return. That's the objective at least, because stocks are purchased for their long-term capital growth potential. However, if the value of the company goes down or stays the same, the stockholder will not be pleased with the investment. The price of a stock is determined solely by what other investors are willing to pay for it.

So you can see that bonds, when compared to stocks, are clearly the safer alternative in most cases. The bond investor is relatively certain what the rate of return will be. The stockholder takes on more risk for a greater potential reward. Bonds are also safer because if the company experiences financial difficulty, bondholders and other creditors are in line to get their money back before stockholders and other owners of the company. However, bonds are limited in their upside potential to the amount of the promised interest rates. Stocks have no limit to the upside and the downside is limited to the amount of the investment.

Advantages: Historically, the best long-term investment, in terms of growth potential, because over time equities earn the highest returns (although, as always, past performance does not guarantee future results). If you have a time horizon of 10 years or greater, equities are *the* place to invest. However, a word of caution is in order. You'll notice that I'm using the plural—equi*ties*. The historical rates of return on equities are an average of the stocks of groups of companies, such as the Dow Jones Industrial Average which

consists of 30 companies, or the S&P 500, which consists of 500 companies. Any one stock within those groupings may lose value over time. Companies are continually going out of business. If you own stock in such a company, you lose your money. Therefore, the potential advantage of owning equities is generally greater through owning stocks in many companies. The problem for individual investors is that they may not be able to afford the broad diversification—stock ownership in many companies and different kinds of companies—necessary to realize returns that match those of market averages. That's one of the biggest reasons that many investors invest in mutual funds, which I address next.

Disadvantages: Stocks are riskier than fixed-interest investments, because no one is promising to pay you anything for the stock. In the short term, stocks can be volatile. Even in the longer term, any one stock may be very volatile.

MUTUAL FUND

The stock market crash of 1929 was caused by millions of investors fleeing the market. In an attempt to bring investors back, Congress created the Investment Company Act of 1940. This act allows Wall Street to create new kinds of companies for the sole purpose of helping the public invest. People buy shares in these investment companies, which in turn hire managers to buy dozens of stocks and bonds in other companies. The profits of each company are then distributed to their respective investors on a pro rata basis. So, if an investment company has assets of $1 million of which $10,000 is yours, you would receive 1% of the profits, consistent with your 1% ownership.

The Investment Company Act of 1940 actually created three types of investment companies. The most popular type was the "open-end fund," which is now known by the more familiar name **mutual fund**. The reason these investment companies are called "open-end" is because they will forever buy and sell their shares. They typically don't close to any investor who wants to get either in or out of an investment. At the time of this writing, there are over 8,000 open-end mutual funds in existence. Mutual funds can be made up of all bonds, all stocks, all cash or cash equivalents, all government securities, or any combination of the above.

Essentially, a mutual fund is an organization that pools the assets of many investors to achieve a common purpose. The money raised is then invested in accordance with predefined goals. This "mutual" effort of a number of investors provides benefits that an individual, working alone, might not be able to receive, such as the following:

• **Professional Management.**

Trained, experienced investment professionals provide research, selection, and monitoring skills needed to manage an investment portfolio.

• **Diversification.** Owning shares in a mutual fund allows investors to participate in a diversified portfolio, instead of placing all of their "eggs" in one "basket." Diversification spreads the risk over many different securities.

• **Convenience.** Mutual funds offer many conveniences. Investment programs can be started with relatively small amounts of money. Dividends and other gains can be automatically reinvested. Many funds offer features to automate both contributions and withdrawals. Regular fund statements ease bookkeeping by tracking an investor's purchases, withdrawals, and reinvestments providing tax information.

Like all equities, open-end mutual funds involve market risk. Both the return and value may fluctuate.

CLOSED-END FUNDS

The second product created by the Investment Company Act of 1940 was "closed-end" funds. Unlike open-end funds, which offer an unlimited number of shares forever, closed-end funds sell only a fixed number of shares. The number is predetermined and does not change. Shareholders who wish to sell cannot return the shares to the fund like open-end mutual fund owners; instead they must seek buyers on the New York Stock Exchange, meaning that the shares are like stocks: they're worth only what another investor will pay for them.

Advantages: Portfolio diversification, professional management, easy market accessibility.

Disadvantages: The internal costs of managing funds can be quite high and tax liabilities can be significant, particularly if the fund has a high turnover, which means that it sells and buys stocks frequently and incurs capital gains on those transactions. Those capital gains are assessed to owners of the fund according to the percentage of the fund they own. Some mutual fund owners have been surprised to find that they had to pay capital gains taxes for their holdings in a mutual fund even in years when the fund lost money. They may have incurred paper losses, but had to pay taxes in real money.

(The third product created by the Investment Company Act of 1940 was the Unit Investment Trust (UIT), which is little used by investors today.)

REAL ESTATE INVESTMENT TRUSTS (REITS)

Real estate can be used as a hedge in an equity portfolio. Real estate enhances the diversity of a portfolio and general-ly has solid growth potential, like equities. Historically, however, real estate has been far less volatile than equities. Investing in individual properties has the potential to yield higher returns. However, this type of real estate investment entails potential liability exposure and management headaches.

Real estate investment trusts (REITs) allow investors to avoid the exposure and the headaches often associated with owning real estate (although not all the market and economic risk). Diversification is generally considered a prudent investment strategy and it's no different with real estate. That's what REITs provide.

A REIT is a trust formed to purchase investment-grade real estate, lease the real estate, and then payout no less than 95% of the income generated. The most conservative programs lease the real estate on a triple net lease basis, which requires that the corporations that lease the properties be responsible for the maintenance, insurance, taxes, and all other expenses of operations.

REITs can provide yields that are comparable to bonds. REITs are available either publicly traded on the stock market or as private non-traded investment trusts. However, unlike bonds, REITs can actually profit from inflation, due to the fact that most triple net leases have escalation provisions tied to the Consumer Price Index. As rents go up, so should dividends, values, and total returns.

In general, real estate took a beating in the late '80s and early '90s. Currently it is widely perceived to be entering an up cycle. However, the performance of a high-quality REIT is not completely driven by the underlying value of the real estate. The escalation provisions, credit worthiness of the tenant, and long-term nature of the leases really drive the performance.

Here's an example. Let's say someone has a new home worth $120,000 and a $1,000 monthly mortgage payment. Let's assume a new nuclear waste disposal site is built next door. The property value depreciates by 50% to $60,000. Does the homeowner get to decrease the mortgage payment to $500? No. The lender is still entitled to $1,000 a month. A quality lease works in a similar manner: the lease payment must be made regardless of the underlying property value. This is not to say that the investor doesn't want values to increase. Any appreciation that occurs benefits the investors. If the REIT sells the property for a gain, the investor also participates in the gain. A REIT, then, is somewhat like a bond in providing ongoing income, but it has the upside potential of real estate appreciation and inflation protection.

Advantages: Real estate can be an effective hedge to an equity portfolio. Due to some limitations on liquidity and historically lower returns than on equities, I typically recommend that investors put only 10% to 20% of their portfolio in real estate.

I rarely recommend bonds to any of my clients, preferring REITs instead for most investors. REITs are better than bonds in my opinion because they provide:

- Potentially higher yields
- Potential tax benefits in the form of depreciation of the underlying property
- Potential appreciation when the property is sold

Disadvantages: Illiquid. Fluctuating returns. Possible loss of principal.

■ ANNUITIES

An annuity is a contract that can guarantee a lifetime income. Usually, it's an agreement between an individual and an insurance company. Annuities can come in many varieties and are distinguished by the nature of their income, premium, payout, and investment alternatives.

FIXED-INTEREST ANNUITIES

A fixed-interest annuity has a predetermined interest rate. Its performance will reflect the prevailing interest rates in the economy. The fixed annuity will have a guaranteed minimum interest rate and the investor cannot have a negative rate of return or lose principal. However, the guarantee relies on the claim's paying ability of the issuing company.

VARIABLE ANNUITIES

If the underlying portfolio determines the investment performance, then the annuity is called a *variable* annuity. Variable annuities typically have a number of different mutual fund-like alternative investment choices called subaccounts. Like mutual funds and other equity investments, a variable annuity does expose the investor to fluctuating returns and potential depreciation of account value.

INDEXED ANNUITIES

An indexed annuity is a hybrid of a fixed annuity and a variable annuity. It closely resembles a fixed-rate annuity but has some growth potential like a variable annuity. An indexed annuity takes a small percentage of the total invested capital and buys options on one or more of the various indices (S&P 500, Dow Jones, etc.). If the index in question appreciates, the investor in turn realizes the appreciation. However, if the index is flat or depreciates, the options expire worthless and the investor gets his or her fixed-interest rate of return on the portion of the total invested capital not used to buy the options.

Any of the above three types of annuities—fixed interest, variable, or indexed—could be classified as either immediate or deferred. Immediate annuities start paying an income immediately after the total contribution is made—and create an immediate tax consequence as well. Deferred annuities don't start paying out until some future date and therefore delay the tax consequences on the earnings until that future date. There are no 1099 tax forms generated and there is no tax liability

until the investor actually takes a distribution from the account. Note that the tax liability, whether immediate or deferred, is at the ordinary income tax rate. Tax deferral is widely regarded as an attractive feature and is a primary reason why an investor would choose to purchase an annuity.

Another perceived advantage of annuities is that they may provide a lifetime income. The payout phase of an annuity can be structured so the investor cannot outlive the income. The investor can also choose a specific amount of income for a specific period of time. These and other "settlement options" give investors the opportunity to create their own pension plan using an annuity contract.

Advantages: Tax deferral and an income stream that cannot be outlived. In Chapter 6, I discuss other strategic advantages of variable annuities.

Disadvantages: Non-qualified distributions are taxed as ordinary income, which for most investors will be at a higher rate than capital gains. Distributions prior to age 59½ may be subject to additional tax penalties. Deferred sales charges may apply. The features within the annuities, such as the death benefit, may result in higher internal fees. The assets do not receive a step-up in basis at the owner's death as some other investments may.

■ PRETAX RETIREMENT PLANS

INDIVIDUAL RETIREMENT ACCOUNT (IRA)

An IRA is the most common type of pretax retirement plan. IRAs are maintained individually rather than by groups and, like all retirement plans, offer two major benefits. First, the amount of your contribution is typically deducted from your adjusted gross income in the year in which you make the contribution. For example, if you've earned $40,000 and are eligible to make a $2,000 contribution to an IRA, the contribution reduces your taxable income to only $38,000. All earnings within the IRA are tax-deferred until you withdraw them.

Contrary to a common misconception, an IRA itself is not an investment, but simply money the U.S. Internal Revenue Code treats differently from other money. There are many investments that can be used inside an IRA to generate a return, including individual stocks, bonds, mutual funds, and the many types of fixed-interest accounts.

Generally speaking, distributions from an IRA are discouraged prior to age 59. Any distributions taken prior to age 59 are generally subject to a 10% early distribution penalty. Mandatory distributions begin at age 70. The penalty for not beginning your distributions properly at age 70 is 50% of the amount in error. In other words, if the correct distribution was $10,000 but $0

was distributed at age 70 the penalty would be $5,000!

Advantages: Reduction of present tax liability. See Chapter 6 for a more complete discussion of pretax retirement plans.

Disadvantages: May increase future tax liability. Inefficient dollars to die with because they will ultimately be subject to income tax for your heirs.

SECTION 401(K) PLAN

The term "401(k)" refers to any profit-sharing or stock-bonus plan that meets certain participation requirements of Section 401(k) of the Internal Revenue Code. To fund the plan, an employee can agree to a salary reduction or to defer a bonus that he or she has earned. Some employers choose to match each dollar put in by the employee with some multiple; e.g., 50%, 75%, etc. Consequently, if the employee does not contribute, neither does the employer.

Individual plan participants may have 401(k) contributions or other additions of up to 25% of after-tax deferral (20% of pretax deferral) income, based on annual gross compensation. The combination of total employer and employee contributions plus any employee deferrals to a participant's account may not exceed $30,000 per year. An employee's elective contributions to the plan are limited to $10,000 in a calendar year (as adjusted for inflation in 1999). Amounts deferred must not violate special nondiscrimination rules.

As with other profit-sharing plans, the funds can generally be withdrawn in the event of termination of employment, death or disability, or attainment of age 59. However, under a Section 401(k) plan, elective contributions can also be withdrawn if the participant has a "financial hardship." Treasury Regulations define this as "immediate and heavy financial need where funds are not reasonably available from other sources." There are "safe harbor" rules that spell out the conditions and requirements for "hardship distributions."

As participants leave the company and separate from the plan, those who are less than 100% vested forfeit that part of the account in which they are not vested. The nonvested forfeitures may then be allocated to the remaining participants. Those participants who remain in the plan the longest will share in the most forfeitures.

Advantages: An easy way to invest. Potential matching contributions from employers.

Disadvantages: Illiquid. May defer taxes to a higher tax bracket. May offer a very limited choice of investments.

SIMPLIFIED EMPLOYEE PLAN (SEP)

A SEP provides an employer with a simplified way to make contributions to an employee's individual retirement account or individual retirement annuity. Employer contributions are made directly to SEP-IRAs set up for each employee with a bank, insurance company, or other qualified financial institution. The employer contributions are tax-deductible and are not taxed currently to the employee. Earnings accumulate income tax-deferred.

The allocation of employer contributions to a participant's SEP account may not exceed the lesser of 15% of compensation or $30,000. For 1999, the maximum amount of compensation considered in this calculation was $160,000. Thus, the maximum allocation to an SEP for an employee was $24,000; for a self-employed individual, the limit was $20,037. The IRS periodically adjusts these limits.

Participants may withdraw or cash out at any time. However, withdrawals are included in taxable income in the year received. Withdrawals prior to age 59 are subject to an additional 10% penalty tax. Exceptions to the 10% penalty apply if distribution is made because of the participant's death or disability or as a series of "substantially equal periodic" payments over the life expectancy of the SEP owner or joint life expectancies of the owner and a designated beneficiary.

Once the periodic payment format is chosen, it may not be modified without penalty before the later of five years, or the participant reaching age 59. An additional exception to the 10% penalty applies for distributions made to pay medical expenses in excess of 7.5% of adjusted gross income. In certain cases, distributions to unemployed individuals for payment of health insurance premiums may also avoid the penalty.

KEOGH PLAN (H.R. 10 PLAN)

Keogh plans are retirement plans for self-employed individuals, e.g., sole proprietors, partners in a partnership, and employees of either type of business. Keogh plans and corporate-sponsored plans differ slightly, by the ways in which they treat life insurance and participant loans.

Distributions prior to age 59 (other than for disability or death) are subject to both a 10% penalty and current income tax. However, if an employee terminates service on or after age 55 or receives a series of substantially equal periodic payments based on his or her life expectancy (or joint life expectancy with a designated beneficiary), the penalty is avoided. For more than 5% owners, distributions must begin when the participant reaches age 70.

Advantages: An easy way to invest. Potential matching contributions from employers.

Disadvantages: Illiquid. May defer taxes to a higher tax bracket.

TAX-SHELTERED ANNUITY (403(B) PLAN)

Employees of religious, charitable, educational, scientific, and literary organizations described in IRC Section 501(c)(3) or public school systems are eligible for 403(b) plans. If past service is ignored, generally up to 1/6 of compensation can be contributed (not to exceed $10,000). If it is desirable to use past service as a contribution base, then it is often possible to exceed the 1/6 limit. However, the rules are very complex and depend on the facts of a specific situation. Other maximums may also be imposed.

Generally the funds are withdrawn at retirement. In order to avoid penalties, withdrawals must begin by April 1 of the year following the calendar year during which the taxpayer became 70 or, if later, the calendar year during which the employee actually retires. At a minimum, the funds must be taken out over the life expectancy of the taxpayer and, if desired, of his or her spouse.

There is a 10% penalty for withdrawals prior to age 59, and all withdrawals are taxed currently as ordinary income unless distribution is rolled over or transferred to another tax-sheltered annuity (TSA) or the annuitant is totally disabled, is separated from service (after age 55), or dies. Also, the salary reduction amount (but not the earnings) is available for "financial hardship," such as an immediate and heavy financial need that cannot be met with other assets.

The transfer of funds from one 403(b) investment to another will not be considered a taxable distribution if the funds remain subject to any distribution restrictions on the prior investment. If a TSA is rolled directly into an IRA, it will defer taxation. If it is paid to the participant first, it will be subject to a mandatory 20% income tax withholding rule.

Advantages: An easy way to invest. Potential matching contributions from employers.

Disadvantages: Illiquid. May defer taxes to a higher tax bracket.

419A(F)(6)

This section of the Internal Revenue Code provides for a welfare benefit plan that enables business owners to obtain special equity-accumulating life insurance for themselves and key employees with pretax dollars. The intent is to fund personal estate tax liability, deferred compensation plans, or corporate buy/sell agreements. The plans created under this section of the tax code are not subject to discrimination testing, meaning that they don't have to be offered to all employees, do not have contribution limits, and may provide survivor benefits that are income tax-free.

Advantages: Tax-deductible. No discrimination testing. Creditor-proof. A great plan for any owner of a closely held corporation who wants to put away more dollars on a pretax basis.

Disadvantages: IRS scrutiny.

NEW IRAS

The Taxpayer Relief Act of 1997 created two tax-favored accounts: Education IRAs and Roth IRAs. Both became available to taxpayers in 1998.

EDUCATION IRA

The Education Individual Retirement Account (Ed-IRA) is designed to help eligible taxpayers save for their children's education. Money contributed to an Ed-IRA is nondeductible and earnings on the account accumulate tax-deferred.

Contributions to a Ed-IRA account are treated as gifts to the beneficiary and, when distributed, are received by the beneficiary free of federal income tax. In general, to the extent that earnings on the account are distributed to pay "qualified" postsecondary educational expenses, the earnings are excluded from the beneficiary's income and are received free of federal income tax. The tax treatments of Ed-IRAs at the state and local level vary. "Qualified" educational institutions include institutions providing education leading to a bachelor's degree or a graduate-level or professional degree. Certain vocational institutions also qualify.

Any earnings distributions not used for qualified higher educational expenses are included in the beneficiary's income and are subject to an additional 10% tax. Certain exceptions apply, including the death or disability of the beneficiary.

If a beneficiary does not use the funds held for him or her in a Ed-IRA, the money may be distributed and rolled over into a new Ed-IRA for a different beneficiary. If the rollover occurs within 60 days of the distribution and if the new beneficiary is a member of the original beneficiary's family (as defined by IRC Section 529(e)(2)), the distribution is not taxable to the original beneficiary. The same objective may be reached by simply changing the beneficiary of a Ed-IRA. As long as the new beneficiary is a member of the original beneficiary's family, the changes are not treated as a taxable distribution.

ROTH IRA

Similar in concept to the traditional IRA, the Roth IRA differs in that contributions are never deductible and, if certain requirements are met, distributions from the account may be received free of federal income tax.

A Roth IRA may be established and funded at any time between January 1 of the current year and the deadline for filing a federal tax return (generally April 15 of the following year), not including extensions. The account must be designated as a Roth IRA at the time it's established.

New IRC Section 408A, which provides for Roth IRAs, allows an existing, traditional IRA (either an annual contribution IRA or a "rollover" IRA) to be converted to a Roth IRA. The taxpayer making the conversion from traditional to Roth IRA must have an adjusted gross income (AGI) of less than $100,000 in the year of the conversion, or no conversion is permitted. The law also prohibits conversion if the taxpayer is using the "married filing separate" status.

The conversion from the "old" IRA to the Roth IRA results in a taxable event: IRA contributions previously deducted and all earnings are added to the taxpayer's gross income on the year the conversion is made. Any 10% excise tax (penalty for early withdrawal) that might apply is waived. If the conversion was done prior to January 1, 1999, the additional income tax due could be paid evenly over four years, rather than in one year.

A wage earner may contribute—but not deduct—the lesser of $2,000 or 100% of compensation earned for the year. If the wage earner is married, an additional $2,000 may be contributed on behalf of a spouse earning less or not working, using a "spousal" account. The family unit may contribute up to a total of $4,000, as long as family compensation is at least that amount. The maximum contribution to a Roth IRA is phased out for single taxpayers with an adjusted gross income between $95,000 and $110,000 and for married couples filing jointly with an AGI between $150,000 and $160,000.

Additionally, the contribution limits for a Roth IRA must be coordinated with those of traditional IRAs. A taxpayer may not contribute more than $2,000 ($4,000 for a married couple) per year into either a single IRA (Roth or traditional) or a combination of IRAs. Excess contributions are subject to a 6% excise tax.

"Qualified distributions" from a Roth IRA are not taxable when received. Qualified distributions are distributions that are made after a five-year waiting period (tax years, not calendar years) and that are made:

- after the taxpayer reaches age 59; or
- in the event of taxpayer's death, or
- because the taxpayer becomes disabled, or
- to pay for "qualified first-time home buyer" expenses (a maximum of $10,000, which must be used within 120 days).

Nonqualified distributions are treated first as coming from the taxpayer's nondeductible contributions (all Roth IRAs are aggregated for this calculation) and are not subject to income tax. Distribution of earnings is included in the taxpayer's gross income in the year received. If taxable distributions are received prior to age 59, a 10% penalty tax may be added.

There are several other significant differences between the traditional IRA and the Roth IRA. Unlike the traditional IRA, contributions to a Roth IRA may be made after the taxpayer has reached age 70. Roth IRAs are not sub- ject to the mandatory distribution requirements (triggered at age 70) that apply to traditional IRAs. Roth IRAs are also not subject to the incidental death benefit rules of IRC Section 401(a), unlike traditional IRAs.

What if you haven't converted your regular IRA to a Roth IRA yet? Should you? Roth IRAs are most appropriate for younger people with a long time horizon or those who have assets that they are quite certain they will never spend and that they want to pass on to their heirs income tax-free.

Advantages: Roth IRAs are tax-free instead of tax-deferred when distributed because the tax on that income has already been paid.

Disadvantages: Illiquid.

■ LIFE INSURANCE

TERM LIFE INSURANCE

Term life insurance, as the name suggests, provides life insurance for a limited period of time, or "term." Additionally, term insurance provides only "pure" insurance protection; it does not have the cash value feature typically found in most permanent life insurance policies.

Term insurance might be compared to an automobile insurance policy. While the auto policy is in force, the insured enjoys protection against loss from an auto accident. If no accident occurs, the policy pays no benefits. At the end of the period covered by the policy, there is no refund of the premiums paid. Term insurance works in much the same way.

Unlike the typical permanent policy, the cost of term life insurance increases as the insured becomes older. The cash value feature usually found in permanent policies provides a build-up within the policy that allows for a constant, level premium. In later years, the cost of the typical term life policy will far exceed the cost of the typical permanent policy.

Decreasing term insurance is term insurance with a level premium and decreasing coverage. This type of term is suitable for covering financial obligations that decrease with time, such as a mortgage or other amortized loan.

Annual renewable term insurance is term insurance with an increasing premium and level coverage. This type of term is suitable for covering financial obligations that remain constant for a short or intermediate period.

Advantages: Much lower cost in the short term than permanent life insurance.

Disadvantages: Must be "lucky enough" to die young for it to be economically efficient.

WHOLE LIFE INSURANCE

Whole life insurance, sometimes called "permanent insurance" or "ordinary life," is designed to stay in force throughout one's lifetime.

Generally, the annual contributions or premiums for this type of policy remain the same throughout the life of the insured. During the early years of the policy, the premiums are higher than those for a straight term life policy. As time passes, the build-up of cash values works with the level premium to keep the whole life policy in force.

If the owner of the policy decides to stop paying the premiums, he or she can terminate the policy and take the built-up cash values minus any potential policy surrender charge. Other options include the purchase of a paid-up policy with a reduced death benefit or a term policy with an equal death benefit but for a limited number of years. The number of years of coverage will depend on the age of the insured and amount of cash value available.

Historically, whole life insurance has provided a number of useful tax benefits, including:

- Tax-deferred build-up of the cash value, which can potentially be distributed income tax-free. The owner can take withdrawals that do not exceed premiums paid as a return of principal that does not trigger a taxable event.

- Loans against cash values at relatively low interest rates and without tax implications. Loans and withdrawals decrease the policy's cash value and death benefit.

- Proceeds generally pass to beneficiaries free of income tax.

Advantages: Competitive investment compared with the "net" return of other fixed-interest investments. More efficient method of acquiring a death benefit than term insurance.

Disadvantages: Potentially low yield compared to variable insurance. Must make a 10-year commitment. Not a competitive return in the short term.

UNIVERSAL LIFE INSURANCE

Universal life insurance contracts differ from traditional whole life policies by unbundling the protection, expense, and accumulation elements. Dividing the policy into the three components allows the insurance company to build a higher degree of flexibility into the contract. This flexibility allows the policy owner (within certain guidelines) to modify the policy face amount of premium in response to changing needs and circumstances.

A monthly charge for both the protection and the expense is deducted from the policy's account balance. The remainder of the premium is allocated to the accumulation element. Because these internal charges are unbundled, complete disclosure is provided to policyholders in the form of an annual statement.

The policyholder has a versatile and flexible tool to accommodate changing business, financial, and family circumstances. Future premiums, based on interest rates and past premiums, may be increased, decreased, or even skipped, without causing the policy to lapse. However, the policyholder assumes more risk than with traditional whole life, because if the accumulation account underperforms, the benefit may be reduced or the premium may be increased to maintain the death benefit.

Advantages: Flexibility of premiums.

Disadvantages: (See "Whole Life Insurance.")

VARIABLE LIFE INSURANCE

Variable life insurance is similar to whole life in that premium payments are level and there's generally a minimum guaranteed death benefit. Unlike whole life polices, however, variable life policies permit the policyholder to allocate a portion of each premium payment to one or more investment options after deduction for expense and mortality charges.

The death benefit and cash value of a variable life policy increase and decrease based on the performance of the investment options chosen. The death benefit, however, will not drop below the initial guaranteed amount, except if the policy premiums are not paid or if loans or other withdrawals are taken from the policy.

Advantages: Upside potential of the stock market.

Disadvantages: Downside potential of the stock market.

VARIABLE UNIVERSAL LIFE INSURANCE

This type of policy contains a combination of features found in *variable* life and *universal* life policies. As with universal life contracts, the owner of the policy can, within certain guidelines, modify the policy death benefit and change the amount and timing of premium payments to meet varying circumstances.

The most prominent feature of the variable universal life contract is the policyholder's ability to direct where net premiums will be invested. The costs for insurance protection and company expenses are deducted; then the balance of the premium goes directly to investment options selected by the policyholder. Options include:

- stocks
- bonds
- real estate
- money market accounts

The ultimate value of the account, at either death or retirement, will depend on the performance of the investment options chosen. Growth is not guaranteed.

As with other permanent life insurance contracts, the owner can borrow against the cash value of the policy. The interest rate charged is generally lower than open market rates. No credit check is required. Any loans or withdrawals will reduce the cash value of the policy and the death benefit.

The Securities and Exchange Commission requires this type of policy to be accompanied by a prospectus, as you would receive for a mutual fund. An individual considering a variable universal life contract should refer to the prospectus for detailed information regarding the policy being offered.

Advantages: Flexible premiums. Creates a strategic "bucket of money" to and from which assets can be repositioned for investing. Upside potential of the stock market.

Disadvantages: Downside potential of the stock market.

QUESTIONS PEOPLE OFTEN ASK ME

I wanted to take your advice on rebalancing my portfolio by asset classes. I decided to do it quarterly, but I discovered that it could be very expensive for me in costs and taxes. What should I do?

You're right: rebalancing often can become complicated, especially for those assets not in tax-deferred plans. Capital gains taxes, surrender charges, back-end loads on mutual funds may all make rebalancing too expensive to do quarterly in many taxable accounts. Of course, if your assets are in tax-deferred plans, you don't have to worry about capital gains. If rebalancing your portfolio quarterly is too expensive, I would recommend rebalancing once a year. It's still in your long-term financial interest to rebalance your account annually to maintain good diversification and asset allocation, even if you incur some costs to do that.

The ease of rebalancing is one of the advantages of variable annuities and variable universal life. Those investment products usually make it easy to transfer money from one subaccount to another within the plan at no cost.

I own several mutual funds. Most are doing well, but a couple are los-ing money or just breaking even. How long should I wait before I get rid of those dogs?

From an asset allocation perspective, I could say, "Every dog has its day." But I won't. How long you hold funds that aren't performing well depends on the reasons you bought them and where they fit in your overall strategy.

Remember that asset allocation and diversification are two keys to longer-term investment success. If you carefully selected those funds to provide a good asset allocation, I would recommend that you be patient—with one caveat. Compare the performance of those funds with others in the same asset class, such as large-cap growth, international, small-cap value. If your funds consistently underperform similar funds that buy assets in the same investment universe and have the same investment goal or philosophy, then you want to consider changing funds. If your funds aren't performing well, but neither are other funds in that asset class—and it's an asset class you want in your portfolio—I'd hang onto them.

To give one example, funds that invested in Japanese stocks lost nearly 20% a year in the mid-'90s. But everything goes in cycles. In the first three quarters of 1999, Japanese funds skyrocketed! It would have been a shame to have weathered a couple years of big losses and finally thrown in the towel just before those funds took off.

Unfortunately, that's what often happens to people who chase the latest and greatest hot fund. If you had a small percentage of your portfolio in a Japanese fund because you wanted international exposure, the losses of those funds in the down years may have been offset by gains in other asset classes. And when they rebounded, they gave a nice boost to the overall performance of your portfolio.

Smart investors look at average performance over a period of time when they allocate assets. I can almost guarantee you that what's hot on the investment scene as you read this will not be the hot thing a year from now. You could try to guess or anticipate trends—and have as many big losers as big winners—or you could play the averages and allocate assets in several different classes and in an effort to get an attractive longer-term return on your investment.

You also want to keep in mind that 75% of mutual funds underperform broader market averages in a typical year. That is a powerful argument for investing a portion of your portfolio in index funds that strive to mirror the performance of the market.

Over the last seven years, the mutual funds in my retirement plan have done very well, but this year they're losing money. I have 60% of my *retirement in aggressive funds. Is that too much? Should I switch to less aggressive funds? I am 55 and plan to retire in 10 years.*

I think you're in a good position. At your age, 60% of your retirement in aggressive funds is not too much, because they have the greatest potential for appreciation and you still have a long time horizon. Markets have ups and downs. I'm sure you're very happy that you invested in aggressive funds for the returns they provided in recent years. Why second-guess that strategy now? It has worked—and it has the potential to work over the long term. One dip in the market is no reason to abandon a successful strategy.

If you were within a couple years of needing that money for living expenses, I'd recommend that you begin to reduce the percentage of your portfolio in aggressive funds—not abandon them, but begin to reduce your percentage in them. But 10 years is long enough that I wouldn't be worried. You may have a down year, but that could be followed by another seven years in which you earn very attractive returns.

I am so tight I squeak when I walk. My money is in bank accounts, with the exception of $10,000 in cash in my sock drawer. I am 60. What should I do? I can't tolerate the notion of losing any of my money.

You have a number of options that are superior in some ways to bank accounts and cash. You could consider money market mutual funds, which have the potential to provide higher returns than bank accounts. You also may want to consider tax-free money market funds. The return will still be quite low, but at least you won't have to pay taxes on those earnings. Bear in mind, however, that CDs and other bank deposits have a fixed interest rate and are FDIC-insured. Money market mutual funds are neither insured nor guaranteed by the U.S. Government and there can be no assurance that they will be able to maintain a stable net asset value.

At age 60, if you're in good health, you still have a life expectancy of more than 20 years, which in investing terms is a long time. In that length of time, average returns on stocks have been fairly steady. Although the value of your investments may drop on any given day, in any week, or even over several months, or years, over many years those investments have the potential to give you an average return superior to those you can earn on fixed-interest investments. But ultimately you have to be able to sleep at night without worrying about your money.

If you can convince yourself to be a little more adventurous, try investing just a little at a time. Perhaps you could invest $2,000 in a conservative mutual fund. See how it feels. You may be able to get comfortable with the ups and downs of the market. And you could still have $8,000 in your sock drawer if that gives you comfort. Then all you have to worry about is a fire or burglary.

I am in my early 80s. When I die, I want my grandson, who is in his 20s, to have my house. How do I go about putting his name on the deed?

You shouldn't do that, for three reasons. One, the value of your house would probably mean that if you gave him half (the effect of putting his name as a co-owner), he may be subject to gift tax on a portion of the value of your home. Two, the value of that gift above the $10,000 gift limitation could be applied against the $650,000 estate tax exclusion when you die. Three, if you make him a co-owner of the house before you die, it could be more expensive for him if he ever wants to sell it. His basis in the house would be its value when you acquired it, which increases the likelihood that he may have to pay capital gains taxes if he sells it.

There's a simple solution. You avoid the problems simply by designating in your will that you want him to have the house. In that case, he would acquire the house for tax purposes at its value when you die, which in most cases would be considerably more than you paid for it. Because he would get that step-up in basis, it's less likely that he would have to pay capital gains, or at least he would pay much less, if he wanted to sell the house at some time. (See the next question.)

My father recently died and I sold his home for $120,000. I just received a 1099 form reporting that amount as income. Do I have to pay income tax on that?

You shouldn't have to. When you file your taxes, you will have to report that 1099 income on Schedule D, but you will also be asked what your basis was in the property, the value when you acquired it, in order to determine if you realized a gain on the sale. In fact, your basis was the same, $120,000, as the price for which you sold the home. The result will be a gain of zero, creating no income tax for that transaction.

You've recommended that we consider the net return of mutual funds rather than just the costs. Is there any exception to that advice? Is there a time when no-load funds have an advantage over load funds?

The mutual funds I would recommend are those that I believe have the potential to provide the greatest net return in their asset class. I do not disqualify a fund from consideration because it has a load, or sales commission, if it provides the possibility of superior performance. I own load funds in my personal portfolio that have provided exceptional returns.

That said, I would recommend funds that have a load, whether front-end (paid when you purchase shares) or back-end (when you redeem them), only for longer-term investments. The load may dilute the net return on your investment in the shorter term, but over time some load funds are worth it: their long-term net return may be superior to the return from no-load funds.

Here's an example of when you should consider only no-load funds. You have a 15-year-old child who is saving for college. Because the money will be needed within three to four years, a no-load fund makes much more sense. Anytime you anticipate redeeming shares within a few years, look at no-load funds.

I just got a statement from my mutual fund company that said I had capital gains and dividends that created a $1,000 tax liability for me. But the fund lost money! In fact, my $50,000 investment has shrunk to $40,000. How is it possible that I have to pay taxes on losses?

It's probably due to *turnover*. Some funds have high turnover, which means they buy and sell many stocks during the year. When they sell stocks for a gain, they have to apportion that gain to their shareholders. Those gains are balanced by any losses they incur when selling stocks. Your tax liability means that they probably sold a lot of stocks that had made money—gains that were not offset by stocks they sold at a loss. Perhaps they are still holding the stocks that decreased so much that the fund value tumbled! They may have also owned a number of stocks that declined in value significantly, but paid fairly high dividends, which are also apportioned to shareholders.

When you're researching mutual funds for taxable investments, the turnover ratio of the fund is something you should consider. Of course, investments in funds through tax-deferred plans incur no such tax liabilities from capital gains and dividends—you simply pay taxes on distributions as income when you take them.

I'm 63 and retired. I have an IRA, but I don't need the income from that IRA yet. Should I delay taking distributions until I have to at age 70?

It depends on your tax situation and the size of the IRA. If you have your IRA in equities that are earning, for example, a 10% return, your IRA will more than double in value between now and the time you have to start withdrawing your money. Will that appreciation push you into a higher tax bracket—that's called "bracket creep"—when you have to start taking distributions? If it's likely to, you may want to begin taking distributions now to the extent that it *won't* put you in a higher tax bracket now, just to reduce the account.

For example, let's say your current (1999) taxable income is $38,000, for a married couple filing a joint tax return, which puts you in a 15% federal tax bracket. Now assume that when you begin taking mandatory distributions, they will push your taxable income above $43,050, which is the 1999 threshold for the 28% tax bracket. To avoid taking those future distributions when they will be taxed at 28% instead of 15%, a considerable difference, you could begin taking distributions now to "soak up" the 15% tax bracket. In other words, you could take a distribution

this year of $5,000 and still be in the 15% tax bracket.

You could use this same strategy at the end of each year between now and age 70 to reduce the size of the IRA at the most advantageous tax rates. This is a strategy you'd probably want to review each December, when you're fairly certain of your income for the year so you can make the right adjustments.

It's not a simple process in many cases, so I'd recommend that you consult someone to help you with the calculations. The IRS permits several methods for determining mandatory distributions.

This strategy is most beneficial for those who are in the 15% bracket, because the jump to the next bracket is so large—to 28%. But even those who are facing the smaller increases between higher brackets—from 28% to 31%, from 31% to 36%, or from 36% to 39.6% (the top bracket)—will still enjoy a considerable tax savings by adjusting their distributions to reduce taxes.

Also keep in mind that IRAs are extremely inefficient dollars to die with because they may be subject to income and estate taxes upon your death—which could eat up as much as 70% of the value of the IRA. This opens up another series of planning challenges and opportunities. If you are relatively certain that you will never need to rely on your IRA for living expenses, you should look as soon as possible at estate planning options that will reduce taxes on your estate.

I recently changed jobs and I don't know what to do with my 401(k) plan from my previous job. Any recommendations?

I have a very strong recommendation: roll over that 401(k) into an IRA. You gain nothing by leaving your money in a 401(k) plan with a previous employer, whether you change jobs or retire. Employers often have considerable discretion in how they run their 401(k) plans—and they may be able to make changes to those plans that are not in your interest. You want control of your money, instead of giving control to a former employer. Moreover, most 401(k) plans offer only a few options for the types of assets you can own in your plan. If your money is in an IRA, you have a very broad universe of investment options. You can choose the ones that best meet your needs—which may not be offered through your plan.

My daughter will begin her junior year of college next year. We had saved enough to pay tuition and expenses for two years, but now we'll have to borrow money to pay for the rest of her education. We're considering borrowing against my 401(k) plan, which our plan permits. I'll essentially be borrowing from myself and paying myself interest. It seems like a good deal. Is it?

No, it's not. For one, your 401(k) is expressly for the purpose of saving for retirement. Borrowing against your

retirement savings should be an absolute last resort. But there's a scarier reason to avoid borrowing from your 401(k).

Although you have every intention of making regular payments and paying off that loan, what if you encounter a financial emergency? What if you lose your job or lose income for any reason and can't make payments on that loan? If you ever default on your loan repayment, the entire amount you borrow is treated by the IRS as an early withdrawal from your retirement plan. The penalties you would have to pay are too high a price. Not a risk I'd like anyone to take, if there's any alternative.

I would recommend that you borrow against any equity in your home before you borrow from your retirement. A home equity loan may be the most efficient way to borrow for many people, because you may be able to take a tax deduction for mortgage interest. You also have the safer option of simply not making contributions to your 401(k) for a couple years and putting that money toward college costs. A final thought: you did well to provide two years of education for your daughter; maybe she should shoulder the responsibility for some of the remaining cost.

I am currently contributing 6% of my gross salary to my 401(k) plan at work, but I need to begin saving more for retirement. Does it make sense to increase my contribution to 10% of my salary?

Probably not. If your employer matches some portion of your contribution, you want to continue contributing enough to earn that match—but I've never heard of an employer that will match up to 10%. Therefore, instead of increasing your contribution, I'd recommend that you consider a Roth IRA as an option. Make as large a contribution to your 401(k) as you need to get the maximum amount your employer will match. Then contribute as much as you can to a Roth IRA, up to the maximum allowed. If you still have money left for retirement saving, then you could increase your plan contribution. Too many people rely too heavily on qualified plans for retirement. A Roth IRA is a great way to diversify your retirement savings. You don't get a tax deduction on your contributions now, but you won't have to pay taxes when you take distributions after the age of 59 either.

Our son is only two, but we want to begin saving for college. Is it best to open an account in my son's name or invest the money in my name?

I believe there are advantages to keeping investments for your child's education in your name. Here are two reasons.

When colleges and universities consider eligibility for financial aid based on need, they will take into account any savings in your child's name, but they will not consider some investments in your name, if structured properly. One example is the cash value of life insurance—which is one reason that I think

variable universal life insurance (VUL) is an excellent vehicle for college savings for parents who are relatively young and healthy. The other advantage of using life insurance to save for college (as well as retirement) is that there are no limits on the amount that can be invested each year, unlike for IRAs and most 401(k)s.

It's a control issue. Under the federal Uniform Gifts to Minors Act (UGMA), money put into such an account comes under the child's control at age 18. (In some states, the child must be 21.) As much as we hope that our children embrace our values, it doesn't always happen. Perhaps when your son is 18 (or 21), he'll decide that what he really wants is a new car rather than a college education. At that point it's his decision, if the account is in his name. If it's in your name, you have the final say in how the money is spent.

The tax benefits of having the account in your son's name are relatively small and should not be the deciding factor.

My son and daughter earn income from baby-sitting for neighbors and doing yard work. I'd like to open a Roth IRA in each of their names. Is that possible?

Yes. The income needed to qualify for a Roth IRA must be earned income and reported on the child's tax return. Be sure you document their earnings.

Will the distributions I take from my IRA count as income in deter-

mining whether my Social Security benefits will be taxed?

Yes. A married couple filing a joint tax return is allowed to earn up to $32,000 before Social Security benefits are taxed. If income exceeds that, 50% of their Social Security benefits are subject to taxation. Even income from municipal bonds counts toward that $32,000 limit, even though those earnings are tax-free.

I am 65 and I have been encouraged to buy life insurance as a way to reduce my taxes. Should I do it?

It's highly unlikely that you'll come out ahead. At your age the internal cost of the insurance will probably be as much as you would save in income taxes. Based on your life expectancy, the insurance company would charge you much more for the death benefit than they would, say, a 30-year-old—which is why life insurance as a tax strategy doesn't make sense for someone your age.

The exception might be if you were buying life insurance for the purpose of providing the money for your heirs to pay taxes on your estate when you die. That's an issue, however, only for those who have an estate worth more than the $650,000 exclusion allowed by the IRS for a single person as of 1999.

I'm 34 and my wife is 32. I have an adjustable life insurance policy. Should I convert it to variable universal life? And if I should, how do I

do it? What would be the tax consequences of doing it?

You appear to be an ideal candidate for a VUL. You can utilize a tax-free exchange of life insurance cash values via IRC Section 1035. Your current insurance agent may be able to help or to introduce you to other policies that may be able to meet your needs.

I have a stockbroker who advises me on investments. Why would I need a financial planner, too?

You may not need both, largely because a financial planner should be able to provide investment advice and in many cases execute those investments—the services your stockbroker provides—and much more. If you get advice on what stocks or funds to buy, but no other planning services, you've already accepted as truth the first myth I addressed in this book: that picking stocks is the key to financial success. I hope that, as you've considered the other topics I've raised, you now realize successful financial planning involves much more than investments. Accounting and tax advice play a central role in an effective financial plan—areas where most stockbrokers do not provide any services.

Investing is perhaps the easiest part of enhancing your financial future. Frankly, it's much easier—and much more fun for most people—to obtain some expertise in picking stocks than to, say, master the intricacies of the U.S. tax code and determine the appropriate, but sometimes obscure, investment vehicles to optimize the efficiency of your money.

I was very fortunate in that I purchased stock in a young company, IBM, long ago and still own it. That stock has increased in value many, many times. My problem now is that if I sell it, I will incur large capital gains taxes. Is there any way to avoid those tax liabilities?

Yes, there is. You could donate the stock to a charitable organization and receive a tax deduction. That donation could take the form of an outright gift or you could create a charitable trust and donate the stock to the trust. The trust could then sell the stock, without paying capital gains, and reinvest the proceeds. The type of trust you establish would depend on whether you need income from those investments. With a charitable remainder trust, the income from those investments would go to you, but the remaining value of the trust's assets would go to the beneficiary organization after a set period of time or upon your death. With a charitable lead trust, the income from those investments would go to the charitable organization, but the remaining assets in the trust would go to your estate upon your death. In either of these instances, you not only avoid capital gains taxes, but also enjoy a tax deduction. And to top it off, your shrewd investment years ago will deliver benefits to a worthy cause of your choosing.

I'm interested in establishing a charitable trust, but I don't know if I have enough money. How much do I need?

Unless you have at least $100,000 to put into the trust, it probably would not be efficient. That's because a trust is a separate legal entity that must file its own tax returns and requires other administrative paperwork. Filing returns and administering the trust will probably cost a minimum of $1,000 a year. With less than $100,000 in the trust, the administrative costs probably would take too high a percentage of the trust's value to justify those costs. Even if your assets wouldn't justify creating a trust, however, an outright gift to the organization of your choice, either while you are living or through your will, would further the interests of the organization and generate a tax deduction for you.

Another option that may work for some donors is a pooled income fund (PIF). Some charitable organizations have created PIFs, which operate like trusts, but combine the gifts of many benefactors.

12 INVESTOR PROFILES

The people in these profiles are not real; however, the situations portrayed are similar to those I've encountered and addressed many, many times over the course of my career. The investment returns included in these profiles are for illustration only and do not represent any specific investment.

DEE AND STU

Ages: 42, 46
Annual income: $95,000
Net worth: $100,000
Goal: Increase savings

When Dee and Stu first became clients of mine, their debt service included: a $130,000 mortgage financed at 8% on a home worth $200,000, a $25,000 car loan recently financed for 4 years at 7.9%, and $5,000 in credit card debt. Their monthly payments were $1,100, $400, and $150 respectively, totaling $1,650.

My advice:

1. Consolidate their debt into a new first mortgage at 7.25%. The advantages seemed obvious. They would achieve a lower interest rate, have deductibility of all the interest (car and credit card interest are not deductible) and extended duration. They

were concerned about the closing costs of 2.5% until we demonstrated the advantages. At 7.25% their new principal and interest payment was $1,120 or $530 less than what they were applying to debt under their previous arrangements.

2. Invest the savings of $530 per month. If they earned a 10% annual return, they would be able to liquidate their entire debt load in about 12 years. However, with such cheap money, we would advise them not to pay off the mortgage even then—and in 30 years they would accumulate over $1,000,000.

AMANDA AND ANDREW

Age: Both 25
Annual income: $43,000
Net worth: None
Goal: Save to buy a home

Amanda and Andrew were both 25 and recently married. Neither pursued any additional education after high school. She worked in a nursing home and he was a mechanic. Together they earned about $43,000 a year. They wanted to have children soon. They were renting but dreamed of owning their own home. They also had credit card debt of about $4,000 at 16% interest and department store debt of $2,000 at 18%. They wanted to start investing $250 a month into mutual funds with us and Amanda was contributing 5% of her salary to a non-matched 403(b) plan at work.

My advice:

1. Don't invest in mutual funds until the debt is eliminated.

2. Apply all discretionary income to paying off the 18% debt. Then when that is gone, pay off the 16% debt.

3. When the debt is gone, create a long-term investment strategy that takes into account the shorter term desires to buy a house and have children.

4. Discontinue contributions to the 403(b). They need that money first to reduce debt and when that is gone to begin to save for a down payment on a house. It doesn't make sense to put money into a 403(b) account that earns 10-12% while paying 16% and 18% on debt.

PHIL AND LIL

Ages: 56, 50
Annual income: $150,000
Net worth: $300,000
Goal: Buy their "dream" home.

You'll recall the couple I referred to in Chapter 4 and Chapter 6 that had enormous credit card debt, which prevented them from buying their dream home, even while they had significant investments in a pretax plan. They finally were able to buy the home they wanted.

My advice:

1. Take a distribution on Phil's 401(k) account. Because Phil was 56 and his $400,000 in a 401(k) was in a dormant account; Phil no longer worked for the company he had the account with. Because of that he could take a distribution from the plan without paying a 10% premature withdrawal penalty. People between the ages of 55 and 59 who have separated from the companies at which they worked to accrue the money, may be able to make withdrawals without any premature distribution penalty. Phil took a $200,000 distribution from the old 401(k), which netted him a little over $100,000 after taxes. (Phil and Lil didn't have enough non-qualified assets to implement any investment strategies to offset the tax liability created by the distribution.)

2. Pay off credit card debt. With the money from the distribution, they paid off their credit card debt, which reduced their debt-to-income ratio sufficiently that they qualified for a loan to buy their dream home.

3. Roll over the remaining $200,000 in the old 401(k) to an IRA that we managed for them. There was no good reason for them to leave their money in the old plan. By converting to an IRA, they gave themselves more investment choices and more

flexibility and removed the third party that had stood between them and their money.

STEVE AND SHARON

Age: Both 56
Annual income: $200,000
Net worth: $4 million
Primary desire: Plan their estate

Steve and Sharon are both 56 and they have a combined net worth of about $4 million. Despite having a significant net worth, they had a number of issues that they want to address. Under current tax codes, they faced estate taxes at the death of the second one of more than $1 million, likely compounding to more than $2 million given their life expectancy. Virtually no money was in Sharon's name. They had amassed more than $2.5 million in qualified plans that would currently be taxed at about 75% including estate taxes, income taxes, and Income with Respect to a Decedent (IRD). Their portfolio included too much of their own company's stock; it was not diversified. They had money invested in corporate and EE Bonds that were not an efficient investment.

My advice:

1. Buy second-to-die life insurance for $2 million of death benefit inside an irrevocable life insurance trust (ILIT).

2. Reposition $750,000 of jointly held assets into Sharon's name so she could use her unified credit.

3. Accelerate distributions from the qualified plans via the IRC 72(t), which allows for distributions before age 59 without a 10% penalty. Furthermore, reposition some of the cash into tax credit real estate and oil/gas for a 90% deduction. Together, the credits and deductions greatly reduce Steve's and Sharon's tax liability on the IRA distributions.

4. Liquidate the majority of the company stock and invest in a broadly diversified portfolio with 80% equity exposure and 20% bonds.

5. Reposition the bonds into a private Real Estate Investment Trust (REIT), increasing the cash flow from 6% to 8% while simultaneously reducing their risk, reducing their taxes, and increasing the upside potential with the expected infusion of capital upon termination of the REIT.

DAN

Age: 42
Annual income: $200,000
Net worth: $1 million
Primary desire: Reduce taxes on stock options

Dan came to us on December 29, 1999 with a problem that he was happy to have. He had become eligible to exercise stock options at his work, but he had to complete the exercise before the end of the year. What possibly could be a problem about exercising options for 20,000 shares that would net $215 a share for a total of $4.3 million income? He was in for a huge tax bill.

Our advice:

1. Prepay his state income taxes on that income. Because state income taxes are deductible on a federal return, prepaying those taxes would reduce his federal tax bill by $130,000.

2. Invest $750,000 in an energy program, which we discussed in Chapter 2. This strategy reduced Dan's tax liability by approximately $335,000.

3. Although we had found a way for Dan to reduce his taxes by $465,000 on the income from the options, Dan's problems were not over. Although he would technically exercise those options in 1999, he couldn't actually have physical possession of the money until January of 2000. So how was he going to prepay his state taxes and invest three-quarter of a million dollars in an energy program? Dan went to the bank and arranged a short-term loan with a favorable interest rate, and Dan got the proceeds of the loan in time to prepay the taxes and make the investment.

INDEX